To Broadway
christian church,
Library ~ GAL 2:10
" Remember,
The Poor "
Pastor Phil

For God so Loved the Inner-City

Urban Missions -
The Forgotten Church Mission Field

Pastor Phil Mortensen

xulon
PRESS

For God so Loved the Inner-City
by Pastor Phil Mortensen

Printed in the United States of America

ISBN 978-1-60477-862-5

www.xulonpress.com

Front and back covers designed by John E. Paul

Table of Contents

Dedication Page

Introduction

The Mortensens --2005

D'Andre Stevenson was not available for this picture

DEDICATION PAGE

Without exaggeration, there are hundreds and hundreds of tremendous people (living and deceased) who have had a great influence on my life and ministry. Space will only allow for a fraction of them to have their names recorded in this book. I am deeply grateful to everyone who has had a vital influence on my life and ministry over the years. I cannot thank you enough.

I want to dedicate this book to the wonderful person who has had the most influence on my life and ministry. That person would be Fran Mortensen, my wife and ministry partner. You believed in me when you were a teenager. I have always appreciated your faith and devotion to me. Although we are two very different individuals, God has made us a real team. You are my best friend and I will always be grateful to God for putting us together and keeping us together through challenging times. I could not do this ministry of showing Christ's love to the poor and needy without you. May God bless you richly in this life and in the life to come.

Love, Phil

A. OBJECTS OF COMPASSION

Palm 106:46

A homeless mother of six children is hiding from the police: sleeping under the Harrison Street Bridge at night. A forty-six year old high school graduate begins to cry at a Bible study because he cannot read. A troubled young man who has spent half of his life behind bars has not received a hug from another human being in over ten years. A mother of five walks her barefoot children through the snow in an effort to receive needed winter clothing. A self-righteous preacher's kid thinks he is better than the poor and needy because he has never been in their shoes. A self-proclaimed racial bigot has to deal with individuals seated in the same row of his inner-city church who come from another racial background. A mentally challenged young man rejoices after receiving a banana in his lunch sack. He had not had any fruit in three months. An inner-city youngster testifies that she knows God loves her because she was fed hotdogs after Sunday school. An inner-city family thanks God for the Christmas presents they received from a generous family living in the suburbs. A rural church family gives an inner-city church family a check for $28,000 so they could purchase a building in the heart of the city of their own.

These brief descriptions are just a few examples of the thousands of lives being touched by God's people through the inner-city ministry of Love Church of Fort Wayne, Indiana. We read in Psalms 106 about a God who looks at a people in distress. He hears their cries and remembers His covenant for their sake. His loving kindness makes them "Objects of Compassion" in the presence of their captors.

All across America we see inner-city communities being taken captive by the unseen enemy who is a thief, destroyer and murderer. The only hope for the inner-city is for God's people to rise up and to put God's Word into practice. New inner-city churches need to be established. There needs to be a greater partnership among urban, suburban and rural churches to advance God's kingdom to every needy person, regardless of their background.

B. PURPOSE SENTENCE

God loves the people of the inner-city and He will provide for those who show them His love.

The purpose sentence above contains nineteen words. It also contains in one sentence what this book is all about. This book is not primarily about a pastor or his wife or his ministry over the past forty years. This book is primarily about God's love for needy people who live in the inner-city communities across our nation.

In the most familiar Bible verse in the New Testament, Jesus tells us in John 3:16 that God so loved the world; and that world includes everyone regardless of race, education level, or class distinction, whether churched or un-churched. The word "so" in English means an indescribable love. God loves everyone. Everyone is made in His image and everyone is made to reflect God's nature and character. I Timothy 2:4 tells us God, *"...desires all men to be saved and to come to the knowledge of the truth."* I Timothy 4:10 describes God as the, *"...Savior of all men, especially of believers."* John 3:17 says, *"For God did not send the Son into the world to judge the world, but that the world might be saved through Him."* I Peter 3:9 says, *"The Lord is not slow about His promise, as some count slowness, but is patient toward you, not wishing for any to perish but for all to come to repentance."* God's love is described all through the Bible in many practical ways. God's love in Matthew 1:21 allows mankind to be saved from their sins. Paul describes Christ's love in II

Corinthians 5:14 as something that controlled him; and in 5:15 gave him a reason to live for Christ. Jesus asked Peter three times in John 21 *"Do you love Me?"* Peter answered and said that he loved Jesus three times; Jesus challenged him to take care of His sheep. I John 3:17 tells us that God's love should lead to meeting the practical needs of others. God's love led Jesus to die for our sins on Calvary.

Proverbs 19:17 makes this promise of Godly provision, *"One who is gracious to a poor man lends to the Lord, and He will repay him for his good deed."* Proverbs 28:27 says, *"He who gives to the poor will never want, but he who shuts his eyes will have many curses."* The King James Version of the Bible says, *"He who gives to the poor will not lack..."* **Think of it!** God identifies Himself with the poor as with no other group of people. The purpose sentence of this publication tells us that God will provide for those who show them [inner-city people] His love.

I will be sharing many examples of how God provides for those who provide for the needs of the people of the inner-city. I have seen first-hand how God provides finances, facilities, food, clothes, workers, strength, purpose, courage and partnership as His Church reaches out in love and obedience in meeting the needs of the poor and needy.

C. DEFINITION OF "INNER-CITY"

What are we talking about when we use the term "inner-city?" I am not a sociologist or a city expert but I will give you my viewpoint. I view the term "inner-city" as relating to the poor and needy individuals of a community. These types of people don't fit with the norm of society. I see the term "urban" applying to the city as a unit. The so-called "Gold Coast" in Chicago is part of the urban community but these people are not economically poor and needy and I would not consider them part of the inner-city. I see "inner-city" people living in various places of our society. They might be migrant workers moving from town to town. People

9

living in depressed areas of a community. Those commonly and degradingly called "trailer trash" may be considered "inner-city" even though they may not be in the heart of a depressed area of a city that we normally associate with the term "inner-city." Homeless people living under bridges; people with severe mental or emotional problems; people living with AIDS; people of lower economic or educational class might also fit this description. In this book I will use the term "inner-city" to refer to the poor and needy, whether they live in the depressed area of a city, the suburbs or rural areas of our country.

Using this definition, Jesus ministered to many inner-city people. He ministered to a despised Samaritan woman who had been married and divorced five times and was living with her boyfriend outside of marriage. Jesus also showed His love and compassion for a woman caught in the act of adultery. In Luke 7:36-50 Jesus showed His unconditional love to a woman who earned her living as a prostitute. He was known as a "friend of sinners" which was a negative term of condemnation by the religious community of His day. He was criticized for ministering to both Jews and non-Jews. He embraced children and physically touched lepers who were considered "unclean" and who were banned to a place outside of the city so no one would be infected by them. In Mark 5:1-20 Jesus ministered to a demon-possessed man living in a graveyard. Jesus praised those who gave alms to support the needs of the poor and needy. Jesus praised the widow who gave all of her limited finances to the Lord. Many of the inner-city people responded positively to Jesus. They received Him gladly. Jesus identified Himself with the poor and needy as His Heavenly Father did in the Old Testament. Praise God that He loves the people of the inner-city and He will provide for those who show them His love.

D. OVERVIEW OF BOOK

This book is broken down into seven major sections and sixteen chapters.

Section I
God's Love for the Inner-City

In Chapter 1 we will examine God's love for the poor and needy from the Old Testament. Chapter 2 deals with God's love for the poor and needy from the New Testament.

Section II
God's Preparation for Inner-City Ministry

We will examine in Chapters 3-6 how God prepared me for inner-city ministry through my family, church, education and failures.

Section III
God's Faithfulness for Inner-City Ministry

In Section III we learn that God is a faithful God and He demonstrates His faithfulness in many ways. Chapter 7 traces God's faithfulness through the marriage of Phil and Fran Mortensen. Satan wants to divide couples in ministry. Though far from being perfect, we'll see how God has put this couple together and used this imperfect couple to show His love to the poor and needy. Chapter 8 examines God's faithfulness through Phil's military service. Chapter 9 highlights God's faithfulness through the 14-year ministry from 1971 to 1985 of Fellowship Bible Church in Fort Wayne. Finally, Chapter 10 features God's faithfulness through Love Church of Fort Wayne from 1986 to the present.

Section IV
God's Truth to Overcome Lies Hindering Inner-City Ministry

There are approximately 1,000 Bible verses from the Old and New Testament that demonstrate God's love and concern for the poor and needy. If that is the case, why is there comparatively little inner-city involvement by the evangelical church today? In Chapter 11 we will examine 15 lies that Christians often believe that hinder inner-city ministry. It is a very thought-provoking section and it will require prayer and openness to profit from it.

Section V
Plan for Effective Inner-City Ministry

What is the hope for the inner-city in America today? Has God forgotten the inner-city with all of its many problems? There is hope. God has a plan for effective inner-city ministry and it is revealed in the Bible. In Chapter 12-we will examine "Development of a Vision for Inner-City Ministry." The truth is that I pastored a church for fourteen years without a vision. I will share how an effective vision was developed that has touched many lives of those living inside and outside of the inner-city. Chapter 13 is entitled: "Partners in Ministry." We will examine three types of partners: Prayer and Accountability Partners; Hands-on Teamwork Partners; and Support Partners. This is a vital chapter for anyone who desires to be used in effective inner-city ministry. Chapter 14 is defined as: "City-Wide Church Relationships." What is the city-wide church? Does the Bible say anything about the so-called city-wide church? How can the city-wide church be used in effective ministry to the inner-city? I believe this chapter will be a great source of encouragement.

Section VI
Summary

Section VI is simply called Summary. We will examine in Chapter 15 "God's Promise of Blessings on Inner-City Ministry." I can tell you personally from God's Word and forty years of ministry that God blesses those who bless the poor and needy.

Section VII
Conclusion

In Chapter 16 we will examine God's challenge as we study "Urban Missions – the Forgotten Church."

I believe God challenged me to write this book on inner-city ministry thirty years ago. I protested by saying, "I'm not a writer." I wrote 130 pages and put the pages away. Recently Pastor Jimi Higgins of Tampa, Florida challenged me with the promise that God would help me tell the story of His heart for the poor and needy through the ministry of Phil and Fran Mortensen.

This book is a less-than-perfect effort to be obedient in challenging God's people to be more effectively involved in inner-city ministry. I have changed some names to protect the identity of some of the people found in the following pages. I have been bothered that there haven't been more books written on the subject of effective inner-city ministry. My prayer is that God would use these pages to get more of God's people involved in this vital ministry of showing God's love and God's heart to the poor and needy within our communities.

SECTION I

GOD'S LOVE FOR THE INNER-CITY

CHAPTER 1

GOD'S LOVE FOR THE POOR AND NEEDY FROM THE OLD TESTAMENT

SCRIPTURES RELATING TO CHAPTER 1

GOD'S LOVE FOR THE POOR AND NEEDY
FROM THE OLD TESTAMENT

Genesis 12:1-3 - *"Now the Lord said to Abram, 'Go forth from your country, and from your relatives and from your father's house, to the land which I will show you; and I will make you a great nation, and I will bless you, And make your name great; And so you shall be a blessing; And I will bless those who bless you, And the one who curses you I will curse. And in you all the families of the earth will be blessed.'"*

Genesis 18:17, 18 - *"The Lord said 'Shall I hide from Abraham what I am about to do, since Abraham will surely become a great and mighty nation, and in him all the nations of the earth will be blessed?'"*

Genesis 22:15-18 - *"Then the angel of the Lord called to Abraham a second time from heaven, and said, 'By Myself I have sworn, declares the Lord, because you have done this thing and have not withheld your son, your only son, indeed I will greatly bless you, and I will greatly multiply your seed as the stars of the heavens and as the sand which is on the seashore; and your seed shall possess the gate of their enemies. In your seed all the nations of the earth will be blessed because you have obeyed My voice.'"*

Deuteronomy 4:37 - *"Because He loved your fathers, therefore He chose their descendants after them. And He personally brought you from Egypt by His great power."*

Jeremiah 31:3 - *"The Lord appeared to him from afar, saying, 'I have loved you with an everlasting love; Therefore I have drawn you with loving kindness.'"*

CHAPTER 1

GOD'S LOVE FOR THE POOR AND NEEDY FROM THE OLD TESTAMENT

"Boy! God was really mad this morning!"

We fixed our sound system so the nursery workers could hear my Sunday morning sermon. After hearing me speak, one of the youngsters in the nursery said "Boy! God was really mad this morning!" I tell that simple story to illustrate a point. I was raised to believe that in the Old Testament God was always in a bad mood. He was always sending judgment, curses, earthquakes and a BIG flood to express His constant displeasure with people. I heard a speaker say once: "If you wear orange sunglasses, everything is going to appear orange. If you wear red sunglasses, everything is going to appear red. If you wear green sunglasses, everything is going to appear green." I want to challenge you to put on your "love sunglasses" and see God's constant love and provision for the poor and needy people in the Old Testament. I was amazed to discover hundreds of Old Testament references to God's compassion for the poor and needy.

Leviticus 19:18 reads, *"You shall not take vengeance, nor bear any grudge against the sons of your people, but you shall love your neighbor as yourself; I am the Lord."* It sounds to me like God must have been in a good mood when He wrote that verse. Of all the hundreds of commands and directives in the Old Testament, the second greatest command of them all was to show God's love to one's neighbor. I guess that includes loving that neighbor who is a heathen and has the world's most obnoxious barking dog.

I heard a man by the name of Mike Pfundstein define a neighbor as "anyone but yourself". I think that's a great definition of the word and what God commands each of us to do. I have the Ten Commandments displayed on my front car license plate. It's very convicting that two of those commands involve my actions concerning my neighbors. I'm much better at not smoking, not drinking, not dancing and not swearing than I am in loving my neighbor.

Let's take a closer look at the word "poor" as it relates to our study. In one sense everyone, compared to Almighty God, is poor and needy. God made each of us with a God-shaped vacuum that only He can fill. One recent definition of the word poor is "resource-challenged". The Bible tells us we all came into this world with nothing and we will leave this world with nothing. We can do nothing without God's help. The person who is more concerned with material goods than with his soul is described as a fool. God created the world out of totally nothing. All of our resources come from God, the provider. It is His love that provides resources for all of His creation. We are all in debt to Him to use wisely the resources He has provided, including provisions for others through us as His people.

The goal of the Christian life is to become more like God in our character, nature, speech, attitude and conduct. Does God really care about the poor and needy? If the answer is "YES"; then I am to reflect God's character, nature, speech, attitude, and conduct as I care about the poor and needy. God's love provided all the needs of His first two children, Adam and Eve. They lacked for nothing. All their needs were met because of the loving nature of their creator. It was God's desire, through His love, to meet all of the needs of His children. His nature to meet the needs of His children has not changed. God is not a God of lack and neither should His children lack anything that His love has provided for them. I love my family and I provide for them as a result of my love for them. Love means provision. We see this provision over and over again, both in the Old Testament and in the New Testament. Let's take a closer look in the Old Testament and see God's loving desire to meet the total needs of His people without regard to race, creed, color or social class.

Love Means Provision

We see in Genesis 1:27 that God created, *"...man in His own image, in the image of God He created him, male and female He created them."* God showed His love in Genesis 1:28 by blessing them and sharing His desire with them. He told them to be fruitful, multiply, fill and subdue the earth. He provided fish, birds and every plant on the surface of all the earth. He provided animals for them. He is a God of love and His love provided for every need Adam and Eve would ever have in their life. God's love provided Adam with a sense of worth and purpose. In Genesis 2:15 he was given the responsibility of taking care of the beautiful Garden of Eden. God could have taken care of the garden Himself. In Genesis 2:19-20 God gave the responsibility of naming all the animals to Adam. God could have named all the animals Himself. **Think of it!** God agreed to whatever Adam called the animals. God called them by the same name. Some have mistakenly believed that work came as a result of sin. Adam was created perfect with a Godly desire to be responsible and fruitful. Satan has done all He can to rob God's creation, especially the poor and needy, from this God given sense of responsibility and purpose. Some have estimated the Garden of Eden to be sixty square miles. God provided Adam with purpose, energy and strength. It is God's desire for everyone to be productive and living with purpose. God's love provided for companionship through the God-ordained institution of marriage and family. Adam had everything but God and His love said in Genesis 2:18 – *"It is not good for the man to be alone; I will make him a helper suitable for him."* Imagine Adam had God all to himself and God said it wasn't enough. God's love is unselfish. God could have said: "Adam has me, what else does he need?" God's love enjoys meeting needs. I love to meet the needs of my family. One of the main reasons God's people are to meet the needs of others is that it brings joy to our Heavenly Father's heart.

God's Love is Unselfish

God's love is concerned for lonely people. God knows that we need Him and that we need companionship. God provides for this need through marriage, family and the church. Exodus 19:6 says: *"and you shall be to Me a kingdom of priests and a holy nation…"* God desires to form a group of individuals into a "holy nation" for His honor and glory. The worst punishment you can give a prisoner is to put him in solitary confinement. Man was not made to be isolated from others. Many of the mass murders committed in our nation over the past few years have been committed by individuals considered to be, by our society, as "loners." People who commit suicide or other acts of violence against society , more often than not, lonely people.

Lamentations 5:1-3 described God's people as strangers and orphans without a father; and mothers without husbands. God was grieved in Job 22:9 when widows were sent away empty and the strength of the orphans was crushed. People from all segments of society struggle with loneliness and isolation. This is even truer in the inner-cities of our nation. People in these depressed areas often lack transportation, education, or the social skills necessary to develop meaningful relationships. The poor and needy are largely isolated from mainstream society. They often live in depressed government housing that many Christians avoid visiting. I visited a lonely lady and she told me that I was the first pastor in twelve years who had ever stepped inside her residence. We pass out bread to lonely inner-city individuals who never have someone from a church visit them. Many middle-class believers have never visited with an inner-city resident. When was the last time you shared a meal with someone from a different race or culture? Our society is becoming more isolated through excessive computer use and other modern means of communication. The average American spends over eight hours a day involved in some form of media. Seventy per-cent of pastors interviewed said they did not have a close friend. We live in an increasingly isolated world. God's love is extended to us so that each of us can overcome loneliness as we reach out to others in need.

God's Love is Very Practical

Not only did God's love provide for needed companionship, it provided for a holy and a healthy sexual union through marriage as found in Genesis 2:23-25. Sexual union within marriage is God's idea. A good healthy sex life within marriage shows God's love to meet a God-given need. God desires to be one with all His people; just as a married man and wife are one with each other in the covenant of marriage. Children are to be a result of such a God-ordained union. This is God's will for all of His creation.

We live in a sex-crazy world that has little regard for what God has to say about the subject. As one rebellious teen-age girl said "I know what the Bible says about sex, but I have my own ideas." That teen-age girl is not alone. She represents the majority of thinking and acting when it comes to sexual activity inside and outside of marriage.

Satan has his own ideas of sexual activity and it has nothing to do with God's prescribed plan found in His written Word. The world has adopted the idea "If it feels good, do it". We have schools giving away condoms to eleven year old children without parental notification. We have seen over 45 million babies aborted since 1973. Millions of people have sexual diseases. The media often portrays sexual activity without any consequences. Young people who have taken a stand of remaining sexually pure before marriage are ridiculed by their peers. In today's society manhood has been reduced to how many sexual conquests he can experience. We are seeing a flood of under-age sexual activity and child abuse.

The inner-city is especially vulnerable to the misuse of sexual activity. Over half of the babies born in the inner-city are born outside of marriage. Over 70% of young men who get their teenage girlfriend pregnant in the inner-city fail to provide for their off-spring. Our government is paying out millions and millions of dollars in welfare assistance to these young mothers. Our society is paying a heavy price for its disobedience to God.

Real Love is a Choice

God's love in the third chapter of Genesis provided Adam and Eve
with a choice to either obey or disobey God and His will for their
lives. Real love is a choice. Adam and Eve made a tragic choice
and every created person since then has shared in the
consequences. Joshua challenged God's people in Joshua 24:15 to
make the right choice. He challenged them to serve the true God
in contrast with the false gods of their day. Choices have
consequences. It is my prayer that God's people, including me,
will demonstrate God's love to others in need. Even after Adam
and Eve's chose to sin against God, we see God's love poured out
toward them. God continued to provide Adam and Eve with the
gift of human life. He could have chosen to strike them dead, but
His love provided them life. God continued to use Adam and Eve
in producing children to populate the world. He provided human
strength for Eve to have babies and for Adam to work the fields of
his day. In Genesis 3:21 God's love provided needed clothes for
both Adam and Eve.

In the fourth chapter of Genesis, God's love provided Adam and
Eve with two sons, Cain and Abel. We all know the story how
Cain killed his brother Abel. God's love in Genesis 4:6 provided
Cain with an opportunity to repent of his evil heart toward his
brother before he killed him. Cain made his choice and became a
murderer. We see God's love for Cain in Genesis 4:15. God
promised to protect Cain from anyone attempting to find him and
kill him. It is so easy to say, "Cain didn't deserve God's love."
The truth is no one deserves His love. I've often heard a
professing believer say: "We tried to help a person from the inner-
city and they didn't even say thank you to us. It was a waste of
time." It is never a waste of time to show God's love to someone
in need of it.

In Genesis 6:13 God was grieved because of excessive violence on
the earth. He still is grieved when His creation suffers from
violence. His people need to get involved in changing the
conditions that often lead to violence. God's people can make a

difference when they show His preventative love to others. When God's people get involved in showing God's love in practical ways, it does make a difference.

There is a great need for God's people to be involved in literacy training. Recent statistics reveal: One out of five high school graduates cannot read his or her diploma; 85% of unwed mothers are illiterate; 70% of Americans arrested are illiterate; 21 million Americans can't read. One person out of every six in the state of Indiana cannot read. It's so easy sitting in a comfortable church and to respond to the pastor's invitation to: "Open up your Bible to such and such a passage." The fact is millions of people are staying away from God's plan for their life because no one will teach them how to read God's Word. Teaching someone to read God's Word is one of the greatest acts of love anyone can do.

Let's see other practical ways God directed His love in the Old Testament. Proverbs 31:12 tells us the Godly woman shows love for her family by providing clothes for her family. The fastest growing ministry within our church family is our free clothes ministry. We had a lady with five children come in one winter day. Her children had no coats, shoes or socks. My grandson took off his socks and offered them to one of the children. I believe one of the greatest blessings in urban ministry is passing that kind of compassion along to our children and grandchildren. Providing good useable clothes is a great way to show God's love to the poor and needy. I am so grateful to Doris Poling and the others who help make our clothing ministry to the poor possible.

Providing food for the needy is one of the greatest ways to show God's love in a very practical way. God said in Exodus 16:32. *"... that they may see the bread that I fed you in the wilderness, when I brought you out of the land of Egypt"* Psalms 37:3 says that as a result of trusting in the Lord and doing good, God will feed His people. God corrected the false leaders for not feeding the flock in Ezekiel 34:8 and feeding only themselves.

God knows that food is an essential part of life. It's ironic, but the first sin committed in the Bible was over food in the Garden of Eden. Esau lost his blessing over food. God used Joseph greatly to help feed his family during a seven-year famine. God used ravens to help feed one of his prophets. Solomon requested God to feed him. God directed the poor to be fed in Isaiah 14:30. God promised in Isaiah 58:14 to feed those who would delight themselves in the Lord. God demonstrated His love to Israel by promising to feed them in Ezekiel 34:14-15.

God Reveals His Love and His Heart

In Genesis 12:1-3, Genesis 18:17-18, and Genesis 22:15-18, when God says He desires to bless everyone on the earth, He reveals His love and His heart. God's love is not for just one class of people or race of people or one nation of people. God is no respecter of persons. It's easy to believe that God loves: "us four and no more." There are over fifteen hundred denominational groups in America.

Our dear people will often stand up and give their testimonies of what God has done for them. They will tell openly how they have been delivered from drugs, improper sex, abuse, alcohol, jail time, poverty and other challenges. I tell them I have them all beat. I am being delivered from excessive religion. I am a recovering Pharisee. I remember the Sunday school pins I used to proudly wear. I've memorized many Bible verses. I am glad I was brought up in the church. Christians have to understand that God is not impressed with our past religious accomplishments. He loves people, even those who are cursing His holy name. He loves our neighbors and wants us to show them His love on a regular basis. He directed His people in Leviticus 19:13 not to defraud one's neighbor. In Leviticus 19:13 we are instructed not to be a talebearer against our neighbor. God says in Psalms 101:5 that He will cut off those who slander their neighbor. Proverbs 14:21 says that the person who despises his neighbor sins. Jeremiah 23:30 pronounces God's judgment against those who steal God's words from their neighbor. God is concerned about our neighbors and so should we.

God's Word tells us in Jeremiah 31:3 that God loves us with an everlasting love. We have seen from the Old Testament how God desires to bless everyone as a practical demonstration of His love. For many years, my wife Fran and I have worked with the poor and needy. We still don't understand it but we know that God has a special love for the poor. He doesn't hate rich people or middle class people but He has a special concern for the poor and needy.

God Has a Special Love for the Poor

In Leviticus 19:10 God instructs His people to leave crops in the field for the poor and for the strangers in the land. Deuteronomy 15:11 says God's people are to: *"...freely open your hand to your brother, to your needy and poor in your land."* In Job 29:16, God identifies Himself as, *"...father to the needy...."* Psalms 34:6 promises that God hears the cries of the poor and delivers him out of his troubles.

God is known as thinking about the poor in Psalms 40:17. Psalms 68:10 says: *"...You provided in your goodness for the poor, O God."* He desires for the poor and needy to praise His name. Psalms

140:12 says that *"God will maintain the cause of the afflicted and justice for the poor."* Proverbs 14:31 is an amazing verse which says: *"He who oppresses the poor taunts his Maker, but he who is*

gracious to the needy honors Him." **Think of it!** The way God's people treat or mistreat the poor actually affects God! Proverbs 21:13 warns that those who shut their ear to the cries of the poor will not be heard by God. God further warns the rich in Proverbs 28:8 not to charge unjust interest in dealing with the poor. God defines the righteous as those who: *"...is concerned for the rights of the poor, the wicked do not understand such concern."* (Proverbs 29:7). The Godly woman in Proverbs 31:20 reaches out her hand to the poor. God promises in Isaiah 41:7 not to forsake the needs of the poor. God tells us in Isaiah 58 that the fast that pleases Him involves sharing our bread with the poor and needy.

Several years ago we did a phone survey with sixty-four area churches. We asked them three questions: Do you feed the poor?; Do you provide clothes for the poor?; Do you provide transportation for handicapped persons to your church services? Out of sixty-four churches, only twenty said they either provided food or knew where food was available to help the poor and only eight churches provided clothing for the poor. Finally out of these sixty-four churches, only one provided transportation for handicapped individuals to attend church services.

The church has made some progress over the years in helping the poor but we have such a long way to go. God is concerned for the sick and the poor. They are much more likely to be sick due to lack of finances for medical needs, medical insurance and medical checkups. The poor have to buy the cheapest food which is also the unhealthiest. The poor often suffer from a lack of exercise. The poor die younger due to neglect and misinformation.

All through the Old and New Testament God's love was expressed for the sick and afflicted. God rose up Hezekiah and gave him a gift of fifteen extra years. God used a prophet to raise a young boy from death. We see God's compassion and love in Isaiah 53 providing healing for the sick. God healed Daniel from his sickness in Daniel 8:27. God judged the false shepherds of Israel in Ezekiel 34:4 for their unwillingness to treat the sick and diseased. I don't understand why and how God chooses to heal certain people and not others in this life. I know God has used sickness as a witness of His grace and purpose in one's life. I also know God's love is the greatest cure through all types of sickness; whether they are spiritual, physical, emotional, mental or social ills.

God's People are to be Agents of His Love to a Sick and Dying World

God's love is to be shown to strangers and those outside of "our group". Exodus 22:21 says strangers were not to be mistreated by God's people who were strangers themselves at one time. Leviticus 19:34 says: *"...thou shalt love Him as thyself, for ye were strangers in the land of Egypt..."* In Numbers 15:29 God's love is offered in the form of forgiveness toward the stranger as well as the nation of Israel. God set up cities of refuge in Numbers 35:15. These were cities for all people, whether they were from the children of Israel or were a stranger who previously had committed a crime could seek refuge. Deuteronomy 1:16 says strangers should be judged fairly as a reflection of God's love and righteousness. God instructed in Deuteronomy 10:18 that the stranger was to be given food and raiment. Ezekiel 47:23 says the stranger should be given his inheritance per God's instructions.

The last word we want to examine from the Old Testament is the word "visit". God shows His love in Genesis 50:24 by visiting His people. Jeremiah 23:2 details Jeremiah's request for God to visit him. In Jeremiah 29:10 God promised to visit His people after they had spent many years in captivity. God visited Hannah in I Samuel 2:21 and she later gave birth to Samuel. God rebuked the false shepherds of Israel in Jeremiah 23:2 for their refusal to visit the scattered sheep under their care.

Love Gets Involved

The word Emmanuel means "God with us". God has chosen to get involved with the needs, sins and concerns of His creation. Love gets involved. God's everlasting love needs to be shown to all people regardless of their background. God has chosen His people to be agents of His love. In Psalms 106:45, God's people are described as: "objects of compassion". As people that have experienced His compassion, we are to show His compassion to others. We are blessed in order to be a blessing.

I hope you still have your "love sunglasses" on and can see from our study of the Old Testament the greater ways of God's love and compassion for all of His creation. Now let's turn to the New Testament and see God's love for the poor and needy in many different ways. He is the same God in both the Old and New Testament. He expects His people throughout all eternity to show His love, and to do so in gratitude for all that the "God of love" has done for us. There is much work to do. Let's see His love in action in the New Testament in Chapter 2 of this study. By the way keep your "love sunglasses" on.

CHAPTER 2

GOD'S LOVE FOR THE POOR AND NEEDY FROM THE NEW TESTAMENT

GOD'S LOVE FOR THE POOR AND NEEDY FROM THE NEW TESTAMENT

John 3:16 - *"For God so loved the world, that He gave His only begotten Son, that whoever believes in Him shall not perish, but have eternal life."*

John 8:28, 29 - *"So Jesus said, "When you lift up the Son of Man, then you will know that I am He, and I do nothing on My own initiative, but I speak these things as the Father taught Me. And He who sent Me is with Me; He has not left Me alone, for I always do the things that are pleasing to Him."*

Acts 10:38 - *"You know of Jesus of Nazareth, how God anointed Him with the Holy Spirit and with power, and how He went about doing good and healing all who were oppressed by the devil; for God was with Him."*

Acts 4:33-35 - *"And with great power the apostles were giving testimony to the resurrection of the Lord Jesus, and abundant grace was upon them all. For there was not a needy person among them, for all who were owners of land or houses would sell them and bring the proceeds of the sales and lay them at the apostles' feet and they would be distributed to each as any had need."*

I John 4:7, 8 - *"Beloved, let us love one another, for love is from God; and everyone who loves is born of God and knows God. The one who does not love does not know God, for God is love."*

I Peter 4:8 - *"Above all, keep fervent in your love for one another, because love covers a multitude of sins."*

CHAPTER 2

GOD'S LOVE FOR THE POOR AND NEEDY FROM THE NEW TESTAMENT

In Chapter 1 we examined God's love for the poor and needy in the Old Testament. We saw a God of compassion who desired to bless all of His creation regardless of class, creed or color. The God of the Old Testament actually commanded His followers to be obedient in showing His love to the poor and needy that lived in that day. God defined righteous people as those who cared about the poor; while the unrighteous lacked such understanding. God was honored when His love was shown to others in need. God warned that people will be cursed who do not show His love to the less fortunate.

We now move to the New Testament and examine God's love for the poor and needy. We need to ask some basic questions.

Question 1

Did Jesus say anything about the need for His followers to show God's love to the poor and needy of His day?

Jesus said in John 10:30 *"I and the Father are one."* When a person looked at Jesus, they were seeing God the Father. Jesus tells us in John 7:28-29 that He came to simply do the Father's will. Jesus said in John 4:34 that doing His Father's will was *"My food."* John 5:18 said the very act of calling God His own Father was making Himself *"equal with God."* He was *"God in the flesh."* He came to show us what His God is really like (Read John 17). According to John 5:18-20 He didn't go anywhere without checking with His Father first. He didn't say anything without getting permission daily from His Heavenly Father according to John 8:28-29. His entire life's focus, according to John 8:29, was pleasing God, the Father. Jesus apparently never got discouraged with the response of the poor and needy to His ministry to them. People through the years often ask me: "Pastor Phil, you never seem to get discouraged working with the poor. How can you do it?" I can truly say the only time I get discouraged working with the poor and needy is when serving them rather than pleasing God becomes my primary focus. I have not been called to convict them, change them, or make them paper members of our church. I have been called to simply love them and trust God to do the changing. The majority of the poor and needy Jesus attempted to help were not repentant or grateful or changed in any outward manner. Jesus did it to honor His Father. We are attempting to honor our Heavenly Father by showing His love to the poor and needy and then to trust Him for any meaningful change. The focus of pleasing our Heavenly Father through showing His love to the poor and needy is one of the keys to long range success and long term sanity while serving God in the inner-city.

Luke 4:18-19 quotes the first words Jesus said following His successful temptation in the wilderness. He said: *"The Spirit of the Lord is upon Me, because He anointed Me to preach the gospel to the poor. He has sent Me to proclaim release to the captives, and recovery of sight to the blind, to set free those who are oppressed, To proclaim the favorable year of the Lord."* In Matthew 5:2-3 we read these words: *"He opened His mouth and began to teach them, saying, 'blessed are the poor in spirit, for theirs is the Kingdom of heaven.'"* In Matthew 11:1-5 we ready the account of some disciples of John the Baptist (who is in prison at that time) asking Jesus the question: *"Are you the expected One, or shall we look for someone else?"* In verse 5 He stated six supernatural proofs of His chosen identity. He concludes with an amazing statement: *"...the poor have the gospel preached to them."* **Think of it!** Preaching the gospel to the poor was equal in the sight of Jesus to healing blind eyes, helping the lame to walk, cleansing the lepers, restoring hearing to the deaf or even raising individuals from the dead. Jesus constantly identified Himself with the poor and needy of His day. Jesus said in Matthew 25:40, *"....Truly I say to you, to the extent that you did it to one of these brothers of Mine, even the* *least of them, you did it to Me."* Jesus taught His followers over and over again about the need for them to show God's love to the poor and needy. Jesus taught in Luke 4:25-30 that God even showed His love to the Gentiles who were in need of it. Teaching about the love of God to heathen Gentiles got Jesus into serious trouble. The Jews in the synagogue angrily responded to His teaching by driving Him out of the city; even attempting to kill Him by pushing Him off a cliff.

A young lawyer came to Jesus asking Him how he could obtain eternal life. Jesus challenged him with these words in Matthew 19:21 *"If you wish to be complete, go and sell your possessions and give to the poor, and you will have treasure in heaven; and come, follow Me."* Jesus used the small gift of a poor widow in Mark 12:42-43 to illustrate real giving. In Luke 7:40-50 Jesus taught on love and forgiveness using a repentant woman who had lived a life of sin and disobedience to God. In Luke 14:7-24, Jesus taught on His desire for the poor, crippled, blind and lame to be invited for a banquet meal; filling what Jesus called *"my house…"* Through His obedient followers Jesus is still inviting the poor, crippled, blind and lame to fill His house.

In Mark 14:1-8, a poor woman came to Jesus and anointed Him with expensive perfume. After this act of love was criticized by others; Jesus responded in verse 9- *"Truly I say to you, wherever the gospel is preached in the whole world, what this woman has done will also be spoken of in memory of her."* Jesus taught His followers using examples of the poor to illustrate truth.

Question 2

How did Jesus demonstrate God's love to the poor and needy of His day?

Jesus taught constantly with His lips and with His life. There are many examples showing the demonstrated love of God to the poor and needy through His son Jesus Christ. Let's begin with the final

35

earthly ministry of Jesus. In Matthew 28: 20 (commonly referred to as the "Great Commission"), Jesus said these words: *"teaching them to observe all that I commanded you; and lo, I am with you always, even to the end of the age."* The two-fold purpose of everything Jesus said and did was to please God and to teach His followers to say and do the same things. I know it is God's will for the church to show God's love to the poor and needy because Jesus said it and modeled it for us to follow. Jesus said in Matthew 6:2: *"So when you give to the poor..."* Jesus did not say: "if you give to the poor..." Jesus expected His followers to give to the poor and promised in Matthew 6:4 that our Heavenly Father would see it and reward those for it.

Jesus showed God's love to a man with leprosy by physically touching him and then healing him according to Matthew 8:1-4. Jesus came in contact with a Roman soldier who was concerned for his paralyzed servant who was fearfully tormented. Matthew 8:5-13 records the healing love of Jesus instantly raising this needy individual. Matthew 9:36 says simply: *"Seeing the people, He felt compassion for them..."* This compassion led to healing forgiveness, deliverance, encouragement, and freedom from fear. It provided physical food, miracles, blessings, preaching, teaching, rest, and other godly results. He showed His Father's love, unconditionally, to all types of people.

Luke 19:1-10 records the love of God shown to a man who was wealthy by worldly standards yet very poor and needy in every other area of human life. His name was Zaccheus and he was a crook, a traitor and a very lonely man. Despite the criticism of others, Jesus showed this unworthy individual God's love through individual attention, truth, forgiveness and restoration. Jesus even offered to spend some time visiting Zaccheus in his home. Zaccheus responded by offering to restore four times what he had defrauded from others in his tax business. In John 8:1-12 Jesus showed the love of Jesus to a woman taken in adultery. According to the law, her sinful act was punishable by death. Jesus was the only one without sin who had the right to kill her. Instead of judgment Jesus extended God's love to her by offering her hope, love and forgiveness. He did not excuse her sin and told her the truth when He said: *"...Go. From now on sin no more."* Once again Jesus endured religious critics who were more concerned about being right in their own eyes than being loving. Time and space in this publication does not allow an examination of all the ways Jesus demonstrated God's love to those in need of it. In summary to the first two questions, let it be said "Yes." Jesus taught His followers to show God's love to the poor and needy by His words and by His loving deeds. We, as obedient followers of Jesus Christ, have no option but to do likewise with our lips and with our lives.

Question 3

How did the early New Testament church demonstrate God's love to the poor and needy?

In order to better answer the question (primarily based on Luke's writings in the book of Acts) we need to examine the make–up of the early New Testament Church. We see people getting together in Acts 2:1-47 who spoke sixteen different languages and lived in Africa, Asia and Europe. The church had more diversity on the first day than most local American church families have two thousand years later. This church was commissioned by Jesus to reach out in God's love to every creature on earth, regardless of class, creed or culture. God's demonstrated love (first demonstrated through the cross of Jesus Christ) was the element that brought them together despite their many differences. God's love further motivated them to meet the felt needs of others. God's love brought them together resulting in, *"...breaking of bread and to prayer"* according to Acts 2:42. Acts 2:44 records the fact that they had all things in common with each other. God's love overcame any selfish desire for independent financial wealth from each other. Acts 2:45 says: *"and they began selling their property and possessions and were sharing them with all, as anyone might have need."* God's love provided for all the needs of the people regardless of their background. How many church leaders could

37

stand up today and honestly say: that, because of the unselfish love of God demonstrated through their people, no one in their church family has any unmet needs? God supernaturally moved on the people with His divine favor and the people walked in love toward each other as a result.

I talked to one pastor who told me he felt the need to announce to his congregation that the following week he would be challenging business men in his church to show God's love to the poor and needy from Acts 2:45. He would challenge them to sell their property and give the proceeds to the church. He received four phone calls that week from top businessmen in his church who threatened to have him fired from his pastoral office if he proceeded with his challenge. He backed off from his challenge. Later he resigned.

I John 2:15 says, *"Do not love the world nor the things in the world. If anyone loves the world, the love of the Father is not in him."* According to Colossians 4:14, Demas was one of the leaders of the early church. Commenting on Demas in II Timothy 4:10, Paul said: *"...Demas, having loved this present world, has deserted me and gone to Thessalonica...."* Recent surveys of the approximately 1,500 pastors who quit the ministry every month in the USA revealed that money was the number one reason they quit. Jesus said in Matthew 6:24 *"No one can serve two masters; for either he will hate the one and love the other, or he will be devoted to one and despise the other. You cannot serve God and wealth."*

We find in the first four chapters of Act that the early New Testament church wasn't perfect but they were largely free from financial greed. It is interesting to note that the first major sin in the church dealt with greed and dishonesty in financial giving (Acts 5:1-11). Peter and John in Acts 3:6 could honestly say, *"I do not possess silver and gold, but what I do have I give to you: In the name of Jesus Christ the Nazarene--walk!"* I heard about a popular national "religious" speaker who charged $35,000 to speak to a state denominational conference; and they paid it. I am sure glad the man who led me to the Lord didn't charge that fee. I would be lost and headed for hell. How many times do we hear non-church goers say about the church: "All they want at that church is money."?

The early New Testament church was falsely charged and persecuted but no one could say they were motivated by greed. In Acts 4:33-37 we see God's abundant grace moving on the people resulting in sold property and human needs met. Barnabas the Apostle owned a tract of land, sold it, and brought the money to the apostles for benevolent distribution. How many pastors have wealthy businessmen in their church who are willing to sell their property to help the poor? I know there are unselfish people but it is a rarity in the American church today.

In Acts 6:1-6 we see the early New Testament church setting up a food ministry, primarily to help widows in need. In Acts 8:1-8 we see the church experiencing persecution and growth at the same time. In Acts 1:8 Jesus said His followers were to go into the whole world including Samaria. Samaria is in between Judea on the south and Galilee on the north. It represents a place where most people don't want to go. In fact, a good Jew would go 100 miles out of his way to avoid Samaria. God raised up a man named Philip who was willing to go to Samaria and proclaim Christ and His love for them. As a result miracles were done and many of these despised people found the Lord. Acts 8:8 says: *"...there was much rejoicing in that city."* The New Testament Church looked beyond racial differences and the entire city was transformed.

Acts 10 records the story of a Gentile man named Cornelius who gave funds to support poor Jews. He was a man of prayer and God directed him to a Jew named Peter. Peter shared his struggle with prejudice against people different than himself. Eventually God used Peter in Cornelius' life and he became a baptized believer. He was the first Gentile convert. We see later in the book of Acts how God's people were used to minister to Jew and Gentile alike.

The book of Acts records the growth of the New Testament church through the preaching of Jesus Christ and the accomplishment of meeting felt needs.

The early Christians knew their greatest witness was their life itself. They were encouraged to be good employees, good providers for their families, and to show God's love to others. God used this church to break down barriers of division between rich and poor, between Jew and Gentile, and between believers and non-believers. As a result, the church grew in numbers and in great influence. These believers endured persecution and suffering. They refused to strike back and refused to selfishly demand their own ways. America in particular is waiting to see such a restored church; full of love and good deeds. I can say from first hand experience that the non-church community will monitor our efforts to see if we are serious about showing God's love to them; showing this love in a variety of meaningful ways. It happened in the book of Acts and it can happen today in America if we are serious about sharing God's love and showing God's love to those who are in need of it.

Question 4

Did the other New Testament writers such as Paul, John, James and Peter have anything to say about our responsibility to show God's love to the poor and needy people living today?

Acts 10:38 says, *"You know of Jesus of Nazareth, how God anointed Him with the Holy Spirit and with power, and how He went about doing good and healing all who were oppressed by the devil, for God was with Him."* Peter, James and John all observed Jesus personally showing God's love to others in need. Paul, when his name was Saul, was asked by Jesus in Acts 9:4, *"...why are you persecuting Me?"* Jesus identified Himself with His people. The way we treat others shows either our love for God or our indifference toward Him. God has promised to be *"...with us...."* as we show His love to others in need. Let's look closer at the writings of Paul, John, James and Peter and see if they say anything about showing God's love for the poor and needy people living today.

The Apostle Paul

We know from God's Word that the Apostle Paul came from a very well-off economic background (See Philippians 3:1-6). Jewish people were taught from the Old Testament to give alms to the poor and the needy. The Holy Spirit led Paul to write many verses regarding God's heart for the poor and needy of his day. In Romans 12:13 we read, *"contributing to the needs of the saints."* Romans 12:20 instructs the believer: *"...if your enemy is hungry, feed him, and if he is thirsty, give him a drink; for in so doing you will heap burning coals on his head."* Verse 21 says: *"do not be overcome by evil, but overcome evil with good."* As a preacher's kid, I heard my father use I Corinthians 16 to encourage people to give of their finances on the first day of the week. Let's look at it closer in verses 1-3: *"Now concerning the collection FOR THE SAINTS (emphasis mine), as I directed the churches of Galatia, so do you also. On the first day of every week each one of you is to put aside and save, as he may prosper, so that no collections be made when I come. When I arrive, whomever you may approve, I will send them with letters to carry your gift to Jerusalem;"* Paul was speaking to the Corinthian church about supporting saints in financial distress in Jerusalem. When the last time was your church took up a major offering to financially support the poor and needy within a church family in another community?

Paul understood according to Titus 3:5, *"He saved us, not on the basis of deeds which we have done in righteousness, but according to His mercy, by the washing of regeneration and renewing by the Holy Spirit."* In the same book, Titus 1:16, says: *"They profess to know God, but by their deeds they deny Him, being detestable and disobedient and worthless for any good deed."* He further writes in Titus 3:1 *"...to be obedient, to be ready for every good deed."*

41

Paul knew there was no clash between God's mercy that saves us and God's mercy that leads us to a life of compassion to those around us in need. The writer of the book of Hebrews writes in 6:10; *"For God is not unjust so as to forget your work and the love which you have shown toward His name, in having ministered and still ministering to the saints."* God is pleased and honored when God's people meet the needs of His people. Paul shared his heart in Galatians 2:10 when he wrote, *"They only asked us to remember the poor-the very thing I also was eager to do."* Galatians 6:10 says these amazing words, *"So then, while we have opportunity, let us do good to ALL PEOPLE, and especially to those who are of the HOUSEHOLD OF FAITH" (emphasis mine).* These verses and many more that Paul wrote stand in contrast to much so-called Christian television programming which says: "Send your money to me exclusively and God will make you rich."

The Apostle John

We know that this man had a special relationship as a disciple of Jesus Christ. As he followed Jesus for three years He saw God's love demonstrated through Him. He wrote in I John 3:1 *"See how great a love the Father has bestowed on us, that we would be called children of God; and such we are."* He wrote about practical examples of God's love in I John 3:16-18. He said: *"We know love by this: that He laid down His life for us; and we ought to lay down our lives for the brethren. But whoever has the world's goods and sees his brother in need and closes his heart against him, how does the love of God abide in him? Little children, let us not love with word or with tongue, but in deed and truth."* John simply states that God's love results in meeting the practical needs of others. I John 4:8 warns: *"The one who does not love does not know God, for God is love."*

III John verses 5-8 define love by thanking the believers for financially supporting traveling leaders who bring them God's truth. John writes in Revelation 2:4-5: *"But I have this against you, that you have left your first love. Therefore, remember from*

42

where you have fallen and repent and DO THE DEEDS you did at first; or else I am coming to you and will remove your lamp stand out of its place-unless you repent (emphasis mine)." I've heard a lot of messages from this great text. John says we repent and turn back to Jesus our first love by doing the deeds we did when we first fell in love with Jesus. Repentance is more than saying: "I'm sorry." A marriage grows cold when each partner stops showing practical ways to express love. Likewise a church family can grow cold and leave its first love when it stops showing practical ways to express God's love.

The Apostle James

The author of the book of James was also the brother of Jesus Christ. The book of James is probably the most practical book of the Bible when it comes to the need of Christians to show God's love to inner-city type people. James 1:27 defines pure religion as, "...visit orphans and widows in their distress, and to keep oneself unstained by the world." In James 2:1-7 we read these convicting words, "My brethren, do not hold your faith in our glorious Lord Jesus Christ with an attitude of personal favoritism. For if a man comes into your assembly with a gold ring and dressed in fine clothes and there also comes in a poor man in dirty clothes, and you pay special attention to the one who is wearing the fine clothes, and say, 'You sit here in a good place,' and you say to the poor man, 'You stand over there, or sit down by my footstool.' Have you not made distinctions among yourselves, and become judges with evil motives? Listen my beloved brethren: did not God choose the poor of this world to be rich in faith and heirs of the kingdom which He promised to those who love Him? But you have dishonored the poor man. Is it not the rich who oppress you and personally drag you into court? Do they not blaspheme that fair name by which you have been called?" James challenges us in James 2:26, "For just as the body without the spirit is dead, so also faith without works is dead." Sadly, there are many "dead" churches in America today. They worship, they sing, they pray, they conduct church business, but there is little or no life because they don't reflect God's heart or God's love to the poor and needy of our day.

The Apostle Peter

This disciple of Jesus Christ was greatly used of God despite his hasty words and inconsistent ways. He wrote his epistles to believers who suffered and were considered as strangers or "aliens" to the world. He referred to God in I Peter 1:17, *"...the One who impartially judges according to each one's work"* Despite their suffering; Peter described God's people as; *"...a chosen race, a royal priesthood, a holy nation, a people for God's own possession,..."* I Peter 2:12 says: *"Keep your behavior excellent among the Gentiles, so that in the thing in which they slander you as evildoers, they may BECAUSE OF YOUR GOOD DEEDS (emphasis mine), as they observe them, glorify God in the day of visitation."* Peter said those that practice good deeds despite their own needs can bring glory to God. I am often asked, "How will a church benefit by helping the poor and needy?" My answer is very simple. Showing God's love to the poor and needy will bring God glory and happiness. An unknown speaker once said: "Our job as Christians is simply making God look good." Romans 2:4 says, *"... the kindness of God leads you to repentance?"* We are not seeing a lot of genuine repentance going on in either God's church or in our nation as a whole. I Peter 3:9 says, *"not returning evil for evil, or insult for insult, but giving a blessing instead; for you were called for the very purpose that you might inherit a blessing."*

We have seen over and over again God's love and care for the poor and needy; both from the Old Testament and New Testament. We see Jesus, who is the Supreme example of God's love to others in need, whether it's spiritual, physical, mental, or any other need. According to Matthew 9:36, Jesus felt compassion for the "inner-city" type of individuals. God directed Him to minister to them. Jesus warned in the end times, according to Matthew 24:12, *"Because lawlessness is increased, most people's love will grow cold."* The word "love" in this verse is "agape" love. Jesus is warning there will come a day when people professing to be God's people will grow cold in the love shown to one another. We cannot allow our generation to grow cold in the love shown to one another. I have seen first-hand that those most willing to show God's love are young people that are raised in materialism. These young people attend integrated schools and interact daily with many different types of young people. Our segregated churches need to reach across man-made lines and truly show God's love to others regardless of race, creed or color. We had an eleven year old boy from a wealthy suburb reluctantly attend our church recently. His grandmother asked him what he thought of our church. He shared: "I liked it because poor people and people of color are welcomed there and they aren't welcome in my church." May God's church always be welcoming those who are in desperate need of God's love regardless of their background.

We have seen that the major writers of the New Testament have much to tell us about God's love and the need for it to be expressed through His Church. Without practical ways of showing God's love, our so-called faith is simply and practically dead. God loves the people of the inner-city. He will provide for those who show them His love according to His Holy Word.

I am often asked: "Pastor Phil, how did you get involved in the inner-city?" I will share in Section II how God used my family, my church, my education and my failures to prepare me for urban mission service.

SECTION II

GOD'S PREPARATION FOR INNER-CITY MINISTRY

SCRIPTURES RELATING TO CHAPTER 3

FAMILY PREPARATIONS

Psalms 37:23, 24 - *"The steps of a man are established by the Lord, And He delights in his way. When he falls, he will not be hurled headlong, Because the Lord is the One who holds his hand."*

Jeremiah 1:5 - *"Before I formed you in the womb I knew you, And before you were born I consecrated you; I have appointed you a prophet to the nations."*

Genesis 50:20 - *"As for you, you meant evil against me, but God meant it for good in order to bring about this present result..."*

I Samuel 16:11 - *"And Samuel said to Jesse, 'Are these all the children?' And he said, 'There remains yet the youngest, and behold, he is tending the sheep.' Then Samuel said to Jesse, 'Send and bring him; for we will not sit down until he comes here.'"*

Exodus 2:15 - *"When Pharaoh heard of his matter, he tried to kill Moses, But Moses fled from the presence of Pharaoh and settled in the land of Midian, and he sat down by a well,"*

Jonah 1:17 - *"And the Lord appointed a great fish to swallow Jonah, and Jonah was in the stomach of the fish three days and three nights."*

Matthew 4:1 - *"Then Jesus was led up by the Spirit into the wilderness to be tempted by the devil."*

Galatians 1:17, 18 - *"...I went away to Arabia, and returned once more to Damascus. Then three years later I went up to Jerusalem..."*

CHAPTER 3

FAMILY PREPARATIONS

Webster's Dictionary gives us some insight into the word "prepare" and the process God uses in our lives known as "preparation". Webster says prepare means to "make ready, usually for a specific purpose, make suitable, fit, adapt, train, to equip or furnish with necessary provisions." God uses an entire series of events (good and bad) to prepare us to serve Him for His service. I have broken down this third chapter to see how God has used my family to prepare me for urban mission service to the inner-city. I will be sharing in Chapter 4 how God used my church background to prepare me for our ministry to the poor and needy. In Chapter 5, I show how God used my educational background to prepare me for urban service. In Chapter 6, I share how God has used some of my many failures in preparation for His ministry through us to the inner-city of Fort Wayne, Indiana.

Family Background of Jesus

Before I share my personal family background, I want us to look at the family background of Jesus. II Corinthians 8:9 says: *"For you know the grace of our Lord Jesus Christ, that though He was rich, yet for your sake He became poor, so that you through His poverty might become rich."* Jesus gave up His heavenly riches and became poor so that He could identify Himself with the poor who received Him gladly. Jesus was literally "born in a barn" because there was no other place for His birth. He was conceived outside of marriage but was blessed with two parents who loved God and desired to do God's will. Luke 2:40 says: *"The Child continued to grow and become strong, increasing in wisdom; and the grace of God was upon Him."* God used 30 years of family and work preparation to prepare Jesus for three and one-half years of earthly ministry. GOD IS A GOD OF PREPARATION:

49

God uses all things in our life and especially our earthly families to prepare us for His divine purpose that He has placed in us. The Psalmist wrote in Psalms 37:23-24 that God prepares our steps, even using our times of falling to teach us that we can depend on Him who holds our hand. Jeremiah 1:5 records how God prepared Jeremiah in his mother's womb before he was born to serve God despite his fears and low self-esteem. Joseph was prepared by God through many trials to fulfill his Godly mission. He was hated by his family, thrown into a pit to die, and eventually sold into slavery by his hateful brothers. Genesis 50:20 says that despite the evil done to him by his family, Joseph saw the hand of God through it all. Samuel was prepared by God in serving Eli. David was prepared to do mighty things for God by faithfully tending a few sheep. Similar to Joseph, David was also mistreated by his brothers.

Despite being the youngest of his family and despite many short comings, David was greatly used of God. God prepared Moses through his time in Egypt and by literally growing up in a palace. Jonah was prepared to serve God even as God prepared a great fish to swallow him up. During the time that Jesus was enduring 40 days of fasting and temptation from Satan the Holy Spirit helped prepare Jesus in His ministry. In Galatians 1:17-18 Paul said God prepared him by sending him into Arabia and other places for three years. God used 40 years in the wilderness to prepare the Children of Israel for the Promise Land. Many of our greatest spiritual leaders today endured times of poverty, persecution, rejection and abuse within their own family. Jesus was misunderstood by His own family members. Thank God that He truly is a God of preparation.

Family of Phil

In order to understand our ministry of showing God's love to the poor and needy we need to examine my family background. As I share about my family, think of how God has used your family in ministry preparation. I didn't come from a "perfect" family but I'm grateful for how God used them in my life.

My father, David Mortensen, was born in Svinning, Denmark on January 30, 1913. He was one of nine children born to a shoe repairman. The Mortensen family left Denmark in 1919 when my father was six years old. My grandparents on my father's side were very strong Christians. They settled in Cedar Falls, Iowa where my dad spent his growing-up years. He quickly learned English. He told me that the hardest thing he learned to do in English was to pray because he thought God was Danish. My father gave his heart to the Lord and felt the call to pastoral ministry. He attended Moody Bible Institute and graduated in 1933. This was at the end of the Great Depression. I remember

that he would tell me stories of working the lunch hour at a famous restaurant in Chicago and making 15 cents an hour plus a candy bar for his pay. My dad played the trombone and he loved music. He also loved to play tennis and enjoyed swimming.

My mother Muriel Powell was born in Badger, Minnesota on July 14, 1913. She was a Methodist preacher's daughter. Her parents really loved the Lord and her father loved to preach God's Word. She told me they had to move about every two years, serving primarily in small towns in Minnesota. She loved to play the piano and she played it beautifully. She gave her heart to the Lord at a young age. She met my father at a Bible conference. They were married in Elmore, Minnesota on April 13, 1936. They eventually lived in Chicago where my father attended and graduated from Northern Baptist Seminary. My brother Calvin David was born in Oak Park, Illinois in 1939. My folks pastored small farming churches in Wisconsin, South Dakota and Minnesota. I was born in Minnesota on Valentine's Day, 1945.

My Dad never made much money but he was well organized and provided for his family. I remember the story he told me how the poor farmers in South Dakota who couldn't give much money to the church would bring pheasants over to show their appreciation. My folks received so many pheasants one year that they had to bury some in the ground at two in the morning lest they would hurt the feelings of the church members who donated them.

My brother and I, along with my sister Mari Joy who was born in 1955, were raised by a father and mother who practiced their faith at home. We were loved and we were disciplined. Proverbs 13:24 says, *"He who withholds his rod hates his son, but he who loves him disciplines him diligently."* My father's "rod" was a wooden spoon. He would tell me: "Son, this is going to hurt me more than it's going to hurt you." I remember driving my bike through the fresh cement in front of the church one day. I told my mother what I had done. She said those terrible words; "Wait till your father comes home. Now go to your room and wait for him." It was a long wait and I had to pay the price for my rebellious ways. My first remembrance of sin was when I took a six pack of cola from a gas station in Detroit. After receiving my spanking, I had to apologize to the gas station owner and that was hard to do.

My Smoking Career

My smoking career began and ended at the age of eight. One day I was trying to impress some older kids (who were almost 10). They had some cigarettes and I told them I smoked. After taking two puffs on this cigarette, I almost choked to death. I returned home and smelled like a tobacco factory. My father smelled the smoke and asked me if I wanted to tell him something. I knew he would kill me if I admitted my unforgivable sin of smoking. I professed my innocence and avoided him the best I could for the rest of the day. My folks would always pray with us before bed time. Before I went to bed that night, my dad asked me the dreaded question; "Son, do you want to tell me something?" I confessed that I smoked a cigarette earlier that day. Instead of giving me a spanking, he asked me a profound question: "Phil, does Jesus want us to smoke?" I replied: "No dad." He then said, "Let's ask Jesus to forgive you for your sin today and for hurting Him." It was a lesson I will never forget. At a young age my father had taught me that the Christian life was simply a matter of pleasing God and asking him for forgiveness when we do wrong. Showing His love to the poor is simply a matter of pleasing Him.

My Father's Priorities

After serving pastorates in several states my family moved to Detroit, Michigan and then from 1951 until 1958 we lived in Pontiac, Michigan. These seven years were the happiest years for my folks. Despite the happy pastorate, my mother suffered greatly with asthma. She would have spells where she could hardly breathe. I remember when we had to get rid of my favorite cat, "Big Ben", because the doctor told my folks cats could contribute to her breathing problems. I personally really enjoyed living in Pontiac. I had lots of friends and was quite popular in junior high.

My father sat me down in late 1957 with some terrible news. He said to me, "Son, we're going to have to move to Denver, Colorado for your mother's health." Denver is the home of a special hospital for individuals with asthma. The climate is considered better than the Midwest because it has lower humidity and many more days of sunshine. I left Pontiac at the age of 12 with bitterness in my heart toward my father because of the move. I was very selfish and I didn't appreciate what my Godly father was trying to do.

My mother's overall health did not improve after we moved to Denver. My attitude toward being in a strange place grew steadily worse. Our new church home was dreadful compared to our church home in Pontiac. I remember our first Sunday at Mount Olivet Church in Denver. I just met a teenage young man who introduced himself as Johnny. He seemed nice and we sat together. Half way through the service he stepped in front of where I was sitting and told me that he had to get out. He literally ran down the aisle and began screaming. I later found out he was having an epileptic seizure. After hearing him scream and lay on the floor of that church; I thought I was living in hell.

My father drove a diaper delivery truck to help with our financial needs. I can still remember the smell of that truck and those dirty diapers in the hot summer weather. I remember the day that I heard my mother crying, which she rarely did. I asked my father "Why is mom crying?" I'll never forget his reply. He said: "She's crying for you son. She knows you don't want to be here. She also knows that our family doesn't appreciate living in Denver, including herself. She feels guilty that she is the reason we are living in a very unhappy place." I asked my dad and my God for forgiveness in regards to my rotten attitude. I never really appreciated at the time what my father, by his example, was trying to teach me. My father's priorities were God first, my mother second, our family third, and the ministry was fourth. Despite the pain, I will always be grateful for the priorities of my father. He faithfully took my mother to the hospital over 90 times for breathing problems. I never heard him or my mother complain about the trials they endured together. I am trying to be a man of similar priorities. I tell our good church folks that they are like Noah. I tell them with humor that God brought Noah forth. Our ministry to the poor and needy is fourth following my priority of loving God, loving my mate and loving my earthly family. I'll never be able to thank God enough for having been raised in a Christian home where a man and wife were people of priorities. My wife Fran and I are trying to do the same in our priorities. It's not easy at times but well worth the effort.

Family Move to Wheaton, Illinois

In late 1961 we were able to leave Denver and move to Wheaton, Illinois. My father had an opportunity to work at Moody Bible Institute in Chicago. It was 32 miles into the city and 32 miles back to Wheaton. My Dad made that trip five days a week for 16 years. He suffered bad headaches but he never stopped serving the Lord. I graduated from high school in 1962 and left for Saint Paul,

54

Minnesota to study to be a radio announcer. My brother and his wife were kind enough to open up their home for me to stay until my training was complete. My sister spent her growing up years in Wheaton graduating from the same school I attended. My folks enjoyed the community and the many Christians that called Wheaton home.

"You've Always Been There for Me"

Many years later I wrote my father a letter and thanked him and mom for always being there for me. My father wanted me to attend Bible college for a year but they supported my decision to leave home at 17 and try and be a radio announcer. My father was there when I asked Jesus into my heart at age eight. He was there to baptize me at the age of twelve. He was there when I received the "Herald for Christ" award at the age of sixteen. My folks were

there when I graduated from High School, military service and college. They were there to support our church ministry even though it was very different from their Wheaton church home. In 1969 my folks, along with my fourteen year old sister, came to Germany where Fran and I were stationed in the U.S. Army. They saved funds for almost two years to make the trip. We visited the little town in Denmark where my father was born. It was a wonderful memory that I will never forget. They held their six-month old grandson Michael in their arms. Michael was born in a U.S. Army hospital in Berlin, Germany. They supported us through good times and bad both in our family and in our ministry. I remember when my dad prayed a prayer of blessing over our first church ministry. It was on the church's tenth anniversary. I understood for the first time the importance of fathers blessing their children. Many years later I spent some time in my parent's home in Wheaton. This would turn out to be the last year of my father's earthly life. Our family had the privilege of attending the

50th wedding celebration of my folks. I was spending some time in the guest room of their home. I heard something down stairs and I couldn't believe my ears. My folks were having an argument. There was no abuse. There was no yelling. I was so blessed to know that my "perfect" parents were having a disagreement with each other. On Friday morning, October 17 my father wrote three words in his diary: "All is forgiven." He went downstairs and dropped dead on the kitchen floor in front of my mother. On January 22, 1990 my mother also went to be home with her Savior, Jesus Christ. She would experience no more trips to the hospital for breathing struggles. One night before the passing of my folks my mother was having a difficult time breathing. We had a brief, unforgettable, conversation at 2:00AM. I asked my mom if she still loved my father after 50 years of marriage. She closed her eyes briefly and said with love to me: "Oh Phil, I love your father so much." My parents gave me riches that no amount of money can buy. I never really cried at their individual funerals because I was so grateful to have had them for my parents. The greatest sermons my dad ever preached had nothing to do with pulpits, pews or church services. My folks lived their sermons every day and literally touched thousands of lives in the process. I have big shoes to fill. I am trying to be an example to my wife, to my two children and my eight grandchildren. With God's help, I will never sacrifice my family upon the altar of my church ministry to the poor. The greatest thing I can do for my church family is to model Christ's love to my earthly family.

God's Priority for Family Ministry

God is a God of priority. God's Word declares in Luke 10:27-28 that loving God with everything we have must be our greatest priority. The second greatest commandment is to love our neighbors as ourselves. The closest neighbors we have happen to be our earthly families. Genesis 18:19 says: *"For I have chosen him, so that he may command his children and his household after him to keep the way of the Lord by doing righteousness and justice so that the Lord may bring upon Abraham what He has spoken about him."* Imagine God's priority for selecting Abraham was so that he could lead his family in the ways of God. Fathers were commanded in Deuteronomy 6:1-7 to teach their children to love God with everything they had. It's not enough to teach Bible information. You can know the Bible without every falling in love with God. I learned to love God primarily by the example my folks set before me. Our children and grandchildren are watching us and the examples we are living.

The Bible is filled with examples such as Eli, who was a successful priest but a failure as a father. David struggled with his children, despite his heart after God. I Kings 11:4 sadly says: *"For when Solomon was old, his wives turned his heart away after other gods; and his heart was not wholly devoted to the Lord his God, as the heart of David his father had been."* Solomon warned his son about getting involved with non-believing women. Unfortunately, Solomon did not follow his own advice and turned away from God. We see many examples of children following the example of unrighteousness set before them.

I Timothy 5:8 says, *"But if anyone does not provide for his own, and especially for those of his household he has denied the faith and is worse than an unbeliever."* Paul further says in I Timothy 3:4-5 *"He must be one who manages his own household well, keeping his children under control with all dignity (but if a man does not know how to manage his own household, how will he take care of the church of God?).* Ephesians 5 tells us that wives are to submit to their husbands as unto the Lord and that husbands are to love their wives as Christ loves His church.

The family is the proving ground for church ministry. My kids aren't perfect but I honestly believe that they have observed parents who are trying to walk out Godly priorities. I thank God for a father who was willing to drive a stinking diaper truck to provide for his family. According to a recent survey, over half of the wives of the men serving in the pastorate wished their husbands had never become pastors. I thank God for a wife who supports me first as a Christian, second as a husband and father, and third as a pastor. I'm blessed to have a true partner in church ministry.

I have not always walked out my priorities but at least I know what they are. I have put church responsibilities ahead of my family at times. I have asked my family to forgive me when I have fallen short. I thank God for their forgiveness and love. By God's grace I'm learning my priorities every day.

How God Has Used my Family to Prepare Me for Our Inner-City Ministry

I have tried to explain my imperfect Christian background. All of us come from an earthly family. I had the privilege of being raised by a Christian couple who lived their faith primarily at home and secondly at church. They supported each other through good times and bad times. I asked my father before his passing what he would do if he had his life to live over. He simply said, "Less rules, more love." We did have a lot of rules but more importantly we had a lot of love shown to us. I remember when we got our first television in the early 1950's. My father placed a large towel on top of the television. He sternly instructed us that we were to cover the screen and turn down the volume if either a beer or a cigarette commercial appeared on the screen. Thankfully that rule was abandoned a few years later. Our home was filled with times of laughter and music. I can remember my mother playing "Overshadowed" on the piano while the canary sang beautifully in the background.

My folks accepted people regardless of class, creed or color. My father worked with pastors from the inner-city many different times. We work with inner-city children who do not have the example I enjoyed while growing up. I never realized how blessed I was to have the parents I did until I began working in the inner-city. I am attempting to pay back my parents for the example they set as I try to live my life as an example to the poor and needy. Each week I get hugs from inner-city children who just want to be shown God's love through me.

CHAPTER 4

Church Preparations

SCRIPTURES RELATING TO CHAPTER 4

CHURCH PREPARATIONS

I Timothy 3:15 - *"...I write so that you will know how one ought to conduct himself in the household of God, which is the church of the living God, the pillar and support of the truth."*

I Corinthians 12:12 - *"For even as the body is one and yet has many members, and all the members of the body, though they are many, are one body, so also is Christ."*

I Corinthians 12:18 - *"But now God has placed the members, each one of them, in the body, just as He desired."*

Acts 4:12 - *"And there is salvation in no one else; for there is no other name under heaven that has been given among men by which we must be saved."*

Revelation 3:20 - *"Behold, I stand at the door and knock; if anyone hears My voice and opens the door, I will come in to him and will dine with him, and he with Me."*

I Corinthians 1:18 - *"For the word of the cross is foolishness to those who are perishing, but to us who are being saved, it is the power of God."*

I Corinthians 1:27 - *"but God has chosen the foolish things of the world to shame the wise, and God has chosen the weak things of the world to shame the things which are strong."*

Romans 10:13 - *"for whoever will call on the name of the Lord will be saved."*

Colossians 1:27 - *"...Christ in you, the hope of glory."*

Philippians 2:16 - *"holding forth the word of life..."*

CHAPTER 4

CHURCH PREPARATIONS

In Chapter 1 and Chapter 2 we have seen many Biblical references in both the Old and New Testament of God's love for the poor and needy. In Chapter 3 we examined the theme of "Family Preparations". We saw how God used the family background of Jesus to prepare Him for effective inner-city ministry to the poor and needy of His day. I shared how being raised in a strong Christian home prepared me for inner-city missions. It's vital that each of us examine our own family background to help us find God's place of ministry.

In Chapter 4, I will share how God used my church background to prepare me for urban mission service. We know if we are honest, we will have to admit that no "perfect" church exists. God has only "imperfect" examples of His love and character to use. I am truly grateful for my church background that God has used greatly in my life and ministry. Let's take a closer look at my church background and perhaps God will give each of us some insight to prepare us for future ministry and service.

Early Church Experiences

I like to joke and say that I was brought to church nine months before I was born. That statement is entirely true. I was born on February 14, 1945 in Blue Earth, Minnesota. Growing up I was known simply as "the preacher's kid" along with my older brother and younger sister. I don't remember anything about Blue Earth other than what my folks told me. They said it was great farm country – home of the Jolly Green Giant. At the age of three we moved from this small community to the big city of Detroit, Michigan. My first memory of church was having punch and cookies in the toddler's class of Gratiot Avenue Church.

At the age of five we moved from Detroit to Pontiac, Michigan. Pontiac is 25 miles northwest of Detroit. My Godly father was asked to be the senior pastor of the Marimont Church which was composed of about 200 folks, mostly hard working factory workers. This church family would shape my spiritual world for many years to come. I can still remember the Marimont Church sign with these words from Philippians 2:16 – *"Holding forth the word of life,.."* The church would best be described as conservative, fundamental, and independent from any other church family. The make up of the men worked in the car factories in Pontiac, like their fathers before them. Few of the women worked outside of the home. Few of the people had a college education as that wasn't important in the minds of the Marimont church community.

The practical ministry philosophy of the church was to have some type of activity going on almost every night of the week. Sunday morning we had Sunday school and Sunday morning service. We had youth group before the Sunday night service followed by singspirations or other activities. Monday night was time for Boys Brigade; Tuesday night was Pioneer Girls; Wednesday night was prayer and Bible study followed by choir practice; Thursday night was calling and visitation; Friday night was class party night; and Saturday was reserved for softball and bowling depending on the time of the year. I can still remember my dad bragging that we only had 2 nights in the entire month without some scheduled church activity. It took a lot of dedication for men working in the car plants to attend the evening activities but many came faithfully. Overall the church treated my folks very well in their seven year stay before we had to move to Denver for health reasons.

The church took a large part of my dad's time schedule. I remember as a young boy when my dad would take 10 minutes out of his busy schedule and hit a tennis ball to me and I would catch it in my glove across the street from the parsonage. The church grew from 200 to almost 400 which meant we needed to expand our physical facility which we did. The majority of the building expansion was done by the skilled men of the church. Our family

life revolved around the activities of the church. My folks loved
the people and I believe the people of the church responded with
their love.

Moving to Denver was a dramatic change from the life we enjoyed
in Pontiac. In January 1958 my father became the pastor of the
Mount Olivet Church located on the east side of Denver. The
church organization was about 20 years old as I remembered with
about 125 in attendance. The Marimont people were fairly happy
and blessed to be together. The Mount Olivet Church was negative
and unwilling to change. The people did not show appreciation to
my folks like they had previously enjoyed in Michigan. There
were a handful of sincere believers but they seemed to be
outnumbered by the negative crowd. Church finances were a
challenge as my father had to work a part-time job to financially
survive. It is very interesting but the make-up of the people was
almost the same as in Michigan: 100% white, middle class people
working in various jobs. The church would also be described as
conservative, fundamental and independent. It was a long three
and one-half years of serving in the Denver church. We enjoyed
many good times in the beautiful mountains surrounding Denver
but the negative spirit of the church was hard to take. It was a
happy day when our family was able to move to Wheaton, Illinois.
My father served as a pastor for approximately 25 years before
going to work performing a wide variety of tasks at Moody Bible
Institute.

My Church Heroes

I was raised in a parsonage for the first 16 ½ years of my life. My
early life was shaped almost entirely by the people who were a part
of the Pontiac and Denver churches that my father pastored. I
would like to list a group of imperfect individuals who would be
classified as my church heroes for their contribution to my life.

David and Muriel Mortensen -They lived their faith seven days a week. They loved their God, their family and their church family in that order.

Evangelist John Linton - God used Rev. Linton to help me invite Jesus Christ into my life at the age of eight. He had a great sense of humor.

Anna Matthews - She was the most patient woman I ever met. She taught children about Jesus. I tested her patience but she never acted in anger. She was still faithfully serving the Lord in her 90's before her passing.

Faithful Sunday School Teachers - People like Mr. Clower, Mr. Weiser, Mr. Case, Mr. Stuart, and many others who faithfully taught God's Word to me.

Bob and Donna Gavette - Bob served as youth pastor for many years. He would open up his home on holidays for young people to hang out and be themselves. Donna Gavette was severely crippled and lived the last years of her life in a wheel chair. I can still see Bob (in my mind) dragging her wheel chair up the front cement steps of our church. This was before wheel chair ramps were in place. I never heard Donna complain. Her favorite song was: "In the Garden." After Donna died in her forty's Bob married a wonderful widow named Wanda. They visited Love Church recently and I was blessed to see them.

Dave and Laura Mae Garlick - Knowing this wonderful couple was the high point of our time in Denver. Dave was our leader of an organization called Boy's Brigade, similar to Boy Scouts. He helped me learn God's Word and was a great example of what a Christian man should be. They had 6 kids who all loved the Lord. Laura Mae was also a great example. Dave helped me earn the "Herald for Christ" pin in 1961. This is similar to an Eagle Scout. Dave helped me feel a sense of success after feeling like a goof-off most of my young life. Boy's Brigade truly influenced my life.

Pastor Jim Richardson - Despite opposition, he taught me about discipleship.

Pastor Jim Clifford – Jim was a gifted evangelist who helped me share my faith confidently with others in need of God's gift of salvation.

Strengths of My Church Background

I would say overall the strengths of my church background far outnumbered the weaknesses. I appreciate the strong Bible foundation of my early years. Every class and almost every church activity centered around God's Word as we knew it to be. Singing hymns and choruses was a great blessing in my youth and still is today. Sincere Christian men and women loved me despite the challenges I gave them. Many good experiences at camp helped me greatly in my Christian walk.

We were raised with what we understood to be strong, Biblical values. We had an understanding of right and wrong. This is in contrast with the relativism of today. We were taught to believe that Jesus Christ is God's only way to eternal salvation as stated in John 3:16, Acts 4:12, Colossians 1:27, Romans 10:9-10, 13, Revelation 3:20 and many other Biblical references. The youth leaders provided wholesome activities such as the good times we enjoyed at Pontiac Lake and canoeing the beautiful AuSable River in Northern Michigan. Thanksgiving, Christmas and Easter centered on God's goodness to us. In contrast, millions of children and young people who are being raised with no Biblical understanding will never understand this goodness. Despite the many strengths of my background, there were also some major weaknesses.

Weaknesses of My Church Background

I feel the best way to share my thoughts on this subject is to number the weaknesses of my church background with a short description of each one:

Everything done outside of the church sphere of influence was "evil."

I got the impression that church-goers were somehow better than those who did not chose to attend church services. Everything outside of church was "worldly" such as the movies, operas, concerts, sports, social clubs, political events, community events, etc. I heard Christians brag that they never read the newspaper because it was "worldly" information. I heard many messages on why this group or that group did not follow Biblical guidelines. "Heathens" were to be avoided at all cost unless they could be immediately converted to our way of thinking and believing. This thinking even involved outward appearance. Young people with long hair and tattoos were to be avoided at all cost. You were expected to "dress up for Jesus" including a tie (Yeah! Like Jesus wore a tie) when you attended a Sunday morning service at our local church.

Anything "fun" must be considered unspiritual or sinful.

Let me illustrate. A young family with five precious little kids began attending our church. They were involved in helping the needy and sincerely appreciated our ministry. One Thursday evening I was teaching and I told a joke to illustrate my point. Humor is a way I communicate God's truth. People with a good sense of humor who love Jesus have had a great influence on me and my ministry. Humor is a good way to minister to the poor and needy in a way they can understand. After I told my joke, the couple with five kids stood up and walked out the door. The husband called me after church and said they would not be back to our church. I asked why and he said he was offended that I would use a joke in my message. He said on the phone: "Jesus never told a joke. The Apostle Paul never told a joke and I will not attend any church that uses humor in the pulpit." As far as I know they are not attending church services anywhere because no pastor would co-operate with their demands to refrain from using humor in their messages.

I can remember my dad saying: "We've had our fun now." We couldn't watch anything on television past 9:00 PM on Saturday because my dad said that it wasn't good preparation for Sunday. I got the impression that Father God was always in a bad mood. God knew when I was sleeping or awake. He knew when I was bad or when I was good. I could never figure out why many so-called "heathens" could have so more much fun than some of the people who attended our church faithfully.

Our church family did not co-operate with most of the other local churches.

I can't recall hearing messages on church unity or co-operation with others. There were many local churches both in Pontiac and in Denver. I can only remember one church in Pontiac that we ever worked with through a musical presentation. The only church in Denver we worked with led to a contest to see who could recruit the highest Sunday morning attendance. The other church won.

For the most part pastors did not get together unless they wanted to hotly debate some particular issue. Pastors didn't get together for prayer and accountability. We didn't understand the Biblical concept of the "city-church" that we will be sharing later in Chapter 13. The Bible speaks repeatedly of such terms as: "one body", "one bride", "one army", "the whole body", "all the saints", etc. We were "independent" of each other and proud of it. We failed to understand the desire of Jesus and His Father for true, Biblical unity as told in John 17. Many of the churches in our fellowship experienced terrible fights and division. As a result many people dropped out of church, as did their children and future grandchildren. Young people would come up to me in junior high and ask me how were the church fights going on in our church family. It was a terrible witness of our faith to those outside of our church family.

Our church family did little to help the poor and needy.

I will never forget one Sunday morning in the early 1970's. While singing in our church choir I observed a young nice looking African-American couple coming in and sitting in the back section of our sanctuary. No one shook their hands or greeted them when they came in. You could see people turning around observing them almost saying with their lips: "What are you folks doing here?" I had just been released from the U.S. Army where I had the experience of working together with men and women from several different racial backgrounds. We worked together for a common cause. Martin Luther King once said: "The most segregated hour in America is 11:00 AM on Sunday in our churches." Our conservative church did not reach across racial lines. We didn't reach out to the poor and needy of any racial group. We sent $10 down to the Rescue Mission once a month because that was their ministry to the poor and needy. We supported missionary work in Africa 8,000 miles away but we couldn't or we wouldn't support African-American churches less than eight miles away. We were racist and didn't even know it. We were strong in foreign missions but very weak in home missions that were right outside our door.

"I Have This Love-Hate Relationship with the American Church."

Ecclesiastes 3: 8 says: *"A time to love and a time to hate."* I have this love-hate relationship with the American Church. Please don't get me wrong. I love God's people but I do hate some of the stuff going on in the church. One local pastor kindly described our church as the church for people who don't like church. I Peter 4:17 warns: *"For it is time for judgment to begin with the household of God, and if it begins with us first, what will be the outcome for those who do not obey the gospel of God?"*

Examine Your Church Background

I have attempted to list some of the major strengths and weaknesses of my church background. I am deeply grateful for how God has used my conservative, evangelical background in my life. I am also grieved with its many weaknesses and its unwillingness to repent of its independence from God. Many sincere believers are choosing to drop out of active involvement in the local church. The percentage of those attending church regularly has steadily dropped for many years in America. I love the church enough to stay and try and make it better. I would encourage you to prayerfully do the same. It has been helpful to list the many strengths and weaknesses that I have observed over the years. Acts 20:28 says that Jesus purchased the church with: *"...His own blood."* God wants to bring needed changes so that we can please Him and influence others for Him.

How God Used My Church Background to Prepare Me for Inner-city Ministry

I would say the number one way God used my background in preparation for inner-city ministry was simply to provide a Biblical foundation. I know from God's Word that God loves the poor and needy that live in the inner-cities of our nation. I know from God's Word that I am to love my neighbor regardless of class, creed or color. I remember the children's song that tells us, "Jesus loves all the little children of the world – red and yellow, black and white, they are precious in His sight." I know it pleases God when we reach outside of our "comfort zone" and show His love in practical ways to others in deep need of it.

I have been blessed with several pastors who have told me that Jesus would probably feel more comfortable attending our inner-city ministry to the poor than a lot of big, fancy church facilities. I humbly agree because of what God has done through our ministry. We give Him all the glory because it is His love and provision that has sustained us over many challenging years of ministry.

Let me give you an illustration to help you understand how God has even used the weaknesses of my background in the church to prepare my heart for inner-city ministry. Suppose a pastor would stand up next week in church and say, "For the next seven days, I don't want anybody to think about bald-headed monkeys." You know people would be thinking about bald-headed monkeys. I say that because I heard messages warning us against associating with other so-called "Christian" groups. The more we were told to stay away the more I wanted to find out for myself what was really wrong with those other groups. Growing up in an all-white church created a hunger to reach out across racial and social lines. It wasn't until I was on active duty in the U.S. Army that I realized that people of various races could love each other and worship together.

I learned a valuable lesson through years: "Acceptance is not agreement." I don't have to agree with someone on every point to accept them as a person in the family of faith. Romans 15:7 says: *"accept one another, just as Christ also accepted us to the glory of God."* I sincerely believe that it brings glory to God when we accept another person in Christ, despite our differences. We can be conservative in our Biblical understanding but liberal in showing God's love to those in desperate need of that love.

In Chapter 5, we'll examine how my educational background played a role in the development of our inner-city ministry. I pray, as you read these pages, that God will give you a greater desire to show His love to inner-city people.

CHAPTER 5

EDUCATION PREPARATIONS

SCRIPTURES RELATING TO CHAPTER 5

EDUCATION PREPARATION

Job 36: 10-12 – *"He opens their ear to instruction, and commands that they return from evil. If they hear and serve Him, they will end their days in prosperity and their years in pleasures. But if they do not hear they shall perish by the sword, and they will die without knowledge."*

Ecclesiastes 12:12 – *"But beyond this, my son, be warned: the writing of many books is endless, and excessive devotion to books is wearying to the body."*

Ecclesiastes 1:18 – *"Because in much wisdom there is much grief, and increasing knowledge results in increasing pain."*

Jeremiah 9:23, 24 – *"Thus says the Lord, 'Let not a wise man boast of his wisdom, and let not the mighty man boast of his might, let not a rich man boast of his riches; but let him who boasts boast of this, that he understands and knows Me, that I am the Lord who exercises loving-kindness, justice and righteousness on earth; for I delight in these things,' declares the Lord."*

John 7:17 – *"If anyone is willing to do His will, he will know of the teaching whether it is of God or whether I speak from Myself."*

II Corinthians 11:3 – *"I am afraid that, as the serpent deceived Eve by his craftiness, your minds will be led astray from the simplicity and purity of devotion to Christ"*

II Timothy 2:15 – *"Be diligent to present yourself approved to God as a workman who does not need to be ashamed, accurately handling the word of truth.*

CHAPTER 5

EDUCATION PREPARATIONS

Acts 4:13 says: *"Now as they observed the confidence of Peter and John and understood that they were uneducated and untrained men, they were amazed, and began to recognize them as having been with Jesus."* This verse has been used as an excuse for Christians not to have to get a formal education to do church ministry for God. None of us will ever enjoy following Jesus around for three and one-half years learning to do ministry as Peter and John were privileged to do.

There are two very different opinions about the importance of formal education to prepare oneself for ministry. One view says education is so vital that no one can be truly used of God without a college degree or a master's degree. The other view says earning a college degree has nothing to do with effective ministry to others.

I take a middle of the road position on the importance of earning a formal college degree. I was privileged to earn a college degree from Fort Wayne Bible College in 1974 (now Taylor University-Fort Wayne) and a master's degree from Huntington College in 1989. Many of these graduates have gone on to effective ministry for the Lord. I have seen others greatly used of God without a formal college education. Earning a master's degree gave me the opportunity to teach urban missions at Taylor University –Fort Wayne. Education like money is a tool that can be greatly used of God for effective ministry to the inner-city community. I don't worship formal college education as an idol but I am grateful for my formal educational background. God used it to help prepare me for effective urban ministry. I would encourage everyone to get as much education as they can obtain. II Timothy 3:7 warns about those: *"always learning and never able to come to the knowledge of the truth."* I John 2:27 tells us our ultimate teacher is the Holy Spirit. Let's look at what God's word says about the subject and how receiving a formal education has been a great tool for urban missions.

Importance of Education to My Family

Education was very important to our family. My dad earned a master's degree from Northern Baptist Seminary in Chicago. My mother earned a teacher's degree and did substitute teaching in Pontiac before my sister was born. My older brother did very well in school. He loved to debate and was awarded a trophy for being the top debating student in the entire state of Michigan while in high school. He later earned his master's degree and doctor's degree from a state university. He has enjoyed success as a speech professor at the University of Wisconsin-Madison for the past 35 years. He has written a number of books in the field of speech and communications. I am very proud of his educational accomplishments. My sister earned her master's degree from the University of Illinois-Chicago. As a successful social worker she has enjoyed her work dealing with many needy people. I am also proud of my sister and her concern for others in crisis.

Dealing with the "Dummy" Lie

Education was not very important to me for many years. I was the middle happy-go-lucky sanguine kid who just liked to have fun. I thought the purpose of school was for meeting girls and enjoying sports. I only failed one course and that was typing. There were 58 girls in the class and another guy and myself. I guess I spent too much time looking at the girls rather than concentrating on developing my typing skills. I was a "C" student and proud of it. Some people would challenge me to "be like your brother" but I wanted to be me. One day my father, in frustration, called me a dummy. It was the only time he used that word on me but it stuck. I saw myself as a dummy incapable of earning good grades. Parents, be careful what you call your kids. They might just believe you and live up to your expectations.

74

There is an old saying which says: "Sticks and stones can break my bones, but words can never harm me." That saying can't be farther from the truth. Words can either do great harm or give great benefit. I've observed how inner-city children use words to put each other down. These unkind words have great effect. I tell people all the time that the lies that Satan and negative people tell you don't get you in as much trouble as the lies that you tell yourself.

The problem was not that my dad called me a dummy once out of frustration. The problem was that I believed the lie that I was a dummy. Proverbs 23:7 says, *"For as he thinks within himself, so he is..."* I heard a civil rights leader say that the average grade for an African-American-Male in the eighth grade that was attending a certain middle school was a "D." That means for every "C" handed out; another student was receiving an "F". No wonder so many inner-city children flunk out of high school. I saw myself as a dummy and my grades reflected it. I was kicked out of middle school for throwing snowballs one day. I graduated from high school with a 1.87 grade point average which is equal to "C".

Addicted to Failure

I took a group of college students downtown to the local Salvation Army. I was showing them a center for homeless men. They offered three hot meals a day, a shower, a decent place to sleep and an opportunity to serve during the day. I asked the leader how long was the program designed for the men to stay. I will never forget what he said when he said: "If we want the homeless men to stay three weeks we tell them it's a six week program. If we want the homeless men to stay three months we tell them it's a six month program." I asked him, "Why do you give the homeless men that response?" He said: "The men we deal with here are addicted to failure. They can't handle success." Why do over 80% of the men prisoners who are released in Indiana return to prison after they are released? The answer is the same. They are addicted to failure. Success has responsibility.

Failure has little responsibility. It's easier to flunk out then to make a real effort. Success breeds success. Failure breeds failure especially in school.

I once asked a school principle how good was he in predicting future failure of a group of first graders that he was observing? He replied that after many years in education, he could observe a group of first graders and could predict within 95-99% of the time who would be a failure and who would be a success. I had wonderful, supportive Christian parents but I still believed the lie that I was a dummy. It is rare to see a loving husband and wife living together in marriage in the inner-city. Fathers were to give their blessing to their children in the Old Testament. It is pretty hard for a father to give his blessing if he is absent from the home. I remember the eight-year old child in our church who wanted to commit suicide because his father was imprisoned for 45 years after attempting to shoot his mother. Most middle class Christian families have no idea of the challenges facing inner-city mothers in an attempt to raise their family without a supportive husband. We will be discussing in Chapter 16 as to how Christians can make a real difference in the educational process of inner-city children and adults without an education.

My Own Educational Struggles

I graduated from Wheaton Community High School in 1962. I never thought I would ever see the inside of a college campus. I attended radio school classes but that was only for about 6 months of night instruction. I had a brief radio career before going to work at a department store in Pontiac, Michigan. I did not see any need for further education. I was just happy working and being me.

I will give more details in Chapter 8, but when I surrendered to God's will in 1969; I told God that I was willing to earn a college degree. I saw a Christian magazine while serving in the U.S. Army. This article listed a number of Christian colleges. The only school that would take a chance on me was Fort Wayne Bible

College located in Fort Wayne, Indiana. They sent me a letter of acceptance and I was enrolled to start school at the age of 25. I still thought of myself as a dummy but I was willing to give it my best shot.

Fran, Michael David (our 18-month old son) and I moved to Fort Wayne, Indiana in August of 1970. The first man we met on campus was Dr. Tim Warner who became the school president in January of 1971. I appreciated his spirit and Dr. Tim remains a dear friend until this day. The G.I. Bill provided necessary finances for me to be a full time student immediately. My first class was psychology and it was taught by a woman named Joan Mayers. She gave me a lot of good advice about college life and life in general. She told all of the freshman that God was giving us a fresh start in a new environment. I appreciated her encouragement.

My wife Fran worked a full-time job to help me get through college. She gave me orders to get nothing less than a "C" if I knew what was good for me. We had to put our young son in nursery school but he did very well. I also worked several part-time jobs to help with the living expenses. The Married Student Fellowship was a real source of encouragement to the married students trying to survive being married and being students at the same time.

The first year, three students- David Keefer, Gene Baker and Keith Van Tilberg, and I formed a gospel quartet called the Redeemed Quartet. Arlene Beard joined us. It was a great experience; singing in a wide variety of churches. We had some  wonderful times together with music and most of all laughter. We experienced an opportunity to see what pastors go through in various congregations.

It wasn't easy but I kept my pledge to Fran to graduate in four years. I was a member of the class of 1974 and proud of it. My family attended the graduation ceremony. I graduated with a 2.65 grade point average which is about a B- average. I will never forget reviewing the graduation program. I notice that only about fifteen of the approximately 150 members of the freshman class graduated in four years. The senior class president came over and said these words to me: "Mortensen, I never thought you would graduate but you made it. Congratulations!" I felt pretty good for being a dummy. I promised myself I would never take another college course but we'll see later that God had other plans.

Master's Degree – Here We Come

It was nice being free for ten years from college obligation. I felt God calling in 1984 to pursue my master's degree from Huntington College (now called Huntington University). They offered a master's degree in Christian Ministry. It took me almost five years to obtain it but God was faithful to me during that time. I was pastoring most of those years while going to school. I also had to work a full-time job to help out with family finances. I had to complete nine courses in my program and that included a lot of reading. I remember being handed my first grade from my first course. I was afraid to look but believe it or not my teacher gave me an "A". It shocked me – maybe I wasn't a dummy after all. God and Fran were very supportive of my advanced education desires. I went on to earn eight more "A's".

I graduated with a master's degree in 1989 with my mom and other family members in attendance. My father passed away in 1986. When they handed me my master's degree, I wanted to stop and point to heaven and remind my Godly father that I wasn't a dummy anymore. It was a very special celebration.

My Educational Heroes

I don't remember much of any class content of the classes I took and passed. I do remember the good people like Dr. Warner and Joan Mayers for their contribution to my life. I have listed a few more of my educational heroes:

Rev. Robert Strubhar - He would often walk me across W. Rudisill Blvd. on our way to chapel. He would put his arm around me and call me "brother".

Dr. Wes Gerig - For his 50 faithful years of service to Christian education. We didn't always agree on theology but he and his wife Mary have always been a source of encouragement and stability.

Dr. Ron Scharfe - He was quiet but I loved his course on I Corinthians.

Mike Davis - He was a supportive friend and counselor to our ministry.

Dr. Wes Willis - He told us that relationships were more vital than grades.

Wayne Widder - He provided valuable insight as we started our first church.

Ira Gerig - He played the organ beautifully always reminding us never to get too sophisticated to sing "Jesus Loves Me".

Joy Gerig and Dick Baxter - For their willingness to listen to me.

Bishop Ray Miller - For his great sense of encouragement in and out of school.

Howard Cherry - For his kindness and encouragement of our own unique ministry.

Dr. Paul Fetters - For giving me the benefit of the doubt passing me on my master's thesis paper.

Examine Your Own Educational Background

Obviously I don't know the educational background of my readers today. All I want to do is challenge my readers to closely examine your own education background. What kind of a student were you? Was school easy or hard for you? Who were some of the teachers that had the most effect on you and why? Did you do your best or did you goof off? Is God calling you to get more education? I remember the 46 year old lady in our church who graduated from Indiana Perdue University-Fort Wayne (IPFW). We are encouraging our people all the time to finish their education regardless of struggle.

How God Used My Educational Background to Prepare Me for Inner-City Ministry

Job 36:10 says in the NAS: "He opens their ear to instruction…" The KJV uses the word discipline in place of the word instruction. Before I graduated my father asked me what Fort Wayne Bible College meant to me. I said in one word it meant the same as my four years in the U.S. Army. That word is simply called discipline. It took discipline to complete my army obligation and it took discipline to complete my college requirements. It also takes discipline to be faithful in any type of ministry but especially in regards to inner-city ministry. One of the main reasons poor people are poor is because they often lack discipline. Anyone serving the Lord in the inner-city must be an example of loving discipline to the people.

80

The book of Proverbs uses the example of the ant to better understand discipline. Solomon further states that those who love to sleep-in will experience poverty. Not all poor people are lazy but it is a major factor of poverty. It is very difficult for many inner-city men to find work once they have a prison record. Living on welfare often hurts one who would desire to live a disciplined life style. It takes discipline to be on a financial budget, to lose weight, to get exercise and to maintain a consistent devotional life.

The inner-city community needs examples of discipline and Christ-like character. I believe God has used my willingness to complete my education to encourage some of our people in their own pursuit of education. My wife Fran has never attended college but she is a great example of Christian discipline. Much to her surprise, Taylor University Fort Wayne awarded her an honorary college degree in 1999 for her many years of faithful Christian service to the inner-city.

I believe earning an education made me a better all-around person. I learned how others believed and practiced. Education expanded my world and introduced me to a wonderful group of people who loved me and supported me. I Corinthians 8:1 says, *"...we know that we all have knowledge. Knowledge makes arrogant, but love edifies."* It is true that some educated people are arrogant and proud. I have also met poor people who are arrogant and proud. We cannot bow down to the idol of education but I know my educational training helped me to be a better husband, father and pastor to the inner-city community. We can learn to accurately handle the word of truth. We don't have to allow our education to lead us astray from the simplicity and purity in our devotion to Christ. We need not to boast in our education but simply in the fact that we are learning to know God and His ways. Education can play a vital roll in that process.

Let's move on the Chapter 6 and see how God uses failure to prepare us for His service. We will look at this subject from both God's Word and my own failures. I trust it will be a blessing to everyone who has ever failed God.

CHAPTER 6

FAILURE PREPARATIONS

Failure Preparations

Genesis 20:2 - *"Abraham said to Sarah his wife, 'She is my sister. Did he not himself say to me, 'She is my sister'? and she herself said, 'He is my brother.'"*

Genesis 26:9 – *"Then Abimbelech called Isaac and said, Behold, certainly she is your wife! How then did you say, "She is my sister?' And Isaac said to him, 'Because I said, 'I might die on account of her.'"*

Exodus 2:11-14 – *"Now it came about in those days, when Moses had grown up, that he went out to his brethren and looked on their hard labors; and he saw an Egyptian beating a Hebrew, one of his brethren. So he looked this way and that, and when he saw there was no one around, he struck down the Egyptian and hid him in the sand. He went out the next day, and behold, two Hebrews were fighting with each other; and he said to the offender, "Why are you striking your companion?" But he said, 'Who made you a prince or a judge over us? Are you intending to kill me as you killed the Egyptian?' Then Moses was afraid and said, "Surely the matter has become known."*

Psalms 51:4 – *"Against You, You only, I have sinned and done what is evil in Your sight..."*

Matthew 26:75 – *"And Peter remembered the word which Jesus had said, 'Before a rooster crows, you will deny Me three times.' And he went out and wept bitterly."*

John 20:24-25 – *"But Thomas, one of the twelve, called Didymus, was not with them when Jesus came. So the other disciples were saying to Him, 'We have seen the Lord!' But he said to them, 'Unless I see in His hands the imprint of the nails...I will not believe.'"*

CHAPTER 6

FAILURE PREPARATIONS

Proverbs 24:16 – *"For a righteous man falls seven times, and rises again, but the wicked stumble in time of calamity."*

Webster defines "failure" as: "The state or fact of being lacking or insufficient; falling short. Not succeeding in doing or becoming. A person or thing that does not succeed." Jesus tells us in John 15:5, *"...for apart from Me you can do nothing." We have all "fallen short"* according to Romans 3:23. Sin has made us all failures in one area of our lives or another.

The Bible is a God-inspired book describing many human failures. The first couple failed by their disobedience to God. The first child born failed later by killing his brother in a fit of anger. Noah failed God by getting drunk. Both Abraham and Isaac failed God by telling lies to protect themselves. Jacob failed by cheating his brother out of a blessing. Moses failed God by murdering a man. Aaron failed God by helping to build a golden calf. David failed God by adultery and murder. Solomon failed God by allowing his heart to be turned away from God. Jonah failed God by running away from the call of God upon his life. Eli failed God by not disciplining his disobedient sons. Peter failed God by denying Jesus three times. Thomas failed God by his unbelief.

Isaiah 53:6 says, *"All of us like sheep have gone astray, Each of us has turned to his own way...,"* Romans 3:23 tells us: *"for all have sinned and fall short of the glory of God."* All the disciples failed the Lord by leaving Jesus during His greatest hour of need. Nine lepers failed to thank Jesus for their healing miracles which they received.

Success vs. Failure

Success of any kind to someone who has been a failure all their life is something to fear and avoid at all cost. Children raised in wealthy homes are raised to be successful. Many inner-city children are practically raised to be failures. Healthy children get their approval in large part from supportive fathers. The inner-city has suffered failure and pain from a lack of supportive fathers. Many inner-city single mothers are making great efforts to raise their children. The simple fact is that it takes two parents to conceive a child and most often two parents to raise the child in order to be successful in later years. A loving church family can never replace a loving biological home but it can have a major influence in how children see themselves and see their Creator and His Son, Jesus Christ.

I have failed the Lord many times in 40 years of ministry. I have learned a great deal from my failures. I want to list 20 major failures (there are many more I could list.) in an honest effort to help my readers to learn from my shortcomings. We have all failed God and God can use our failures to make us successful in His service if we are willing to learn from them. Let's briefly examine the 20 major failures I have committed and see how God has used them.

Failure # 1 – Not having a clear vision to know where I was going.

I saw a bumper sticker that read: "Don't follow me – I'm lost." We will talk more about the importance of having a vision for inner-city ministry in Chapter 12. Let me just say at this time that no ministry should ever be started without believing in a clear vision of where God is leading them. I heard a former pastor tell how he pastored for 14 years without a vision. I couldn't believe anyone could pastor for 14 years with a vision but this was exactly what I did at Fellowship Bible Church. I saw vision as something binding, restrictive, legalistic and something that I wanted to avoid. I am blessed that Love Church was started with a vision that we are walking out daily 21 years later. I learned the hard way that I needed to have a vision. Our vision is more than a slogan or something nice to put on a church business card. It is the reason why we are on the earth at this time. Having a vision is liberating, Godly and Biblical. I've learned from the major failure of not having a vision. I encourage every believer to seek God based on His Word to find out God's vision for their life and ministry.

Failure # 2 - Trying to recruit people by either being a people-pleaser or by being a legalist.

This is personally one of the greatest failures of my life. If you don't have a vision, you have to be a people-pleaser or a legalist. Galatians 1:10 says: *"For am I now seeking the favor of men, or of God? Or am I striving to please men? If I were still trying to please men, I would not be a bond-servant of Christ."* The Bible is full of people-pleasers that get people to follow them for their own selfish purposes. A legalist (like the Pharisees) is someone trying to put man-made rules on their followers in an effort to earn the favor of God. Jesus loved people but He was not a people-pleaser. According to John 8:28-29 (two of my favorite verses), Jesus did everything to please God. He fought with the legalists of His day who were trying to place heavy burdens on the people that they were unwilling to bear themselves.

Failure # 3 – Making a deal to put a man in a high leadership position on the false assumption that we both could use each other to selfishly promote ourselves.

II Peter 2:3 (KJV) describes false teachers as those who make "merchandise" out of their followers. People in the inner-city community know the meaning of the word "prostitute". Someone uses a prostitute for their own selfish purposes. I am not proud of it and God has forgiven me but I have prostituted or used people for my own selfish purposes. There is a saying in the world that goes: "I'll scratch your back if you scratch my back." God doesn't make deals and He doesn't expect His leaders to make deals either. Jesus served people; others used them for their own selfish purposes. I can't describe the pain I have caused myself and others because of the deals I made in our first church ministry. I Corinthians 12:18 (KJV) says: *"But now hath God set the members every one of them in the body, as it hath pleased Him."* We have to trust God to bring us people for whom please God is the only reason to be with us. I can honestly say I am not aware of using any person for selfish reasons since Love Church began. I learned a hard lesson through failure number three and I do not ever want to repeat it.

Failure # 4 – Asking someone to assume the role of a leader before they first proved themselves worthy of being a leader.

I Timothy 3:6 warns about putting a new convert into a high leadership position. It is easy to select someone for leadership based on personality, talent, financial status or ability. I have been amazed to hear the testimonies full of zeal from baby-Christians. It is impressive to hear how God has saved someone from a life of drugs, alcohol or prison. It is easy to put a new believer into leadership especially if they are gifted in music and make the pastor look good. Many pastors have failed to find out personally how a person acted in their previous church experience. I have learned the hard way to personally contact the former pastor and tell the pastor that a previous member of their church is interested in being involved in our church. Even secular employees know the value of this practice. Failing to find out if a person is faithful before leadership will bring headaches.

Failure # 5: Believing the lie that I could not internally hear from God or be lead by God through His written Word.

God's Word encourages us over and over to listen to God's internal voice placed within a person's spirit. God promises to lead and guide us. He further promises to confirm His direction and His will for their life and ministry for those who earnestly seek Him. The problem in my life was that I didn't believe God could or would speak to me internally and lead me by His written Word. This lie led to other lies such as so-and-so leader is more spiritual than me or that God loves some leader more than me. A good leader must have confidence that they can internally hear from God and be lead by God's written Word. I was tormented for many years believing lie number five. God never promises anything that He can't fulfill. Praise God for His voice and His Word.

Failure # 6 – Believing the lie that someone else could internally hear from God for me.

Failure number five leads to failure number six. If a person believes they cannot hear from God; they will find someone who can hear from God on their behalf. As evangelicals, we believe in the priesthood of the believer. Everyone who has a personal relationship with Jesus Christ has been called to be His priest. I panicked and found a leader who I thought was more spiritual than me and could hear from God better on my behalf. I do not blame anyone but myself but failure number six led me to lose my ministry and position as pastor of Fellowship Bible Church. It was a very hard lesson to learn.

Failure # 7 – Believing the lie that if things fall apart-I could blame my leader.

Ever since Adam and Eve, people have been looking to someone else to blame for their own failures. I was hiding behind my leader. I was guilty of the sin of failing to lead. I was a coward blaming others for my failure to lead. God's people need to be led. God leads through imperfect leaders-that's the truth.

<u>Failure # 8 – Not listening well to the wise counsel of my wife who loves me.</u>

In many ways it is far more challenging to be a pastor's wife than to be a pastor. She receives more criticism and it hurts far deeper than many pastors. I believe in accountability and I have been involved in accountability groups for years with a wonderful group of Christian men. Their love, support and correction has been a great blessing. The problem is they don't get to see me on a daily basis the way my wife, Fran, gets to see me. Sometimes the male ego is not receptive to the input of a loving wife. God's Word says my wife is my "help-mate" and God knows I need help. Fran is not always right in what she says or how she says it but I am slowly learning to listen better to her.

<u>Failure # 9 – Believing a lie that I could not remain in office if someone left our ministry.</u>

I want to give a strong word of advice especially to young pastors. No matter how capable you are, no matter how hard you try, someone is going to leave your ministry on either good terms or bad terms. I remember when our first assistant pastor moved out of state on good terms. As a result, I really did not think I could survive without him. Sometimes people leave churches on bad terms and that is hard to go through. Ask yourself this question – "Who called me to the ministry – God? Or people?" God always provides for what He orders. People will come and go. Thank God for people who love us and support us. Don't ever forget our calling is to God first and people second.

<u>Failure # 10 – Believing a lie that a certain person was my source of financial support.</u>

God uses giving people to help maintain church finances. We have had some wonderful givers to help maintain our ministry over the years. The lies come in when we believe that a certain giving person is our source of financial support. The truth is God is our source of everything we need. Too many pastors have allowed financial pressure to make them forget the source of their finances.

Failure # 11 – Believing a lie that I would be happy in ministry if we reached a certain attendance figure.

Several years ago, Fran and I had the privilege of visiting the Province of Labrador in eastern Canada. We traveled the only paved road linking eight small villages that totaled 3,000 residents between them. I noticed there was a gospel-preaching church in every village. Snow piles up to 15 feet deep there during very cold and long winters. I thought about the faithful pastors who may see 15-20 people in church on any Sunday morning. American pastors are constantly challenged to attend this seminar if they want to grow a big church. I am not opposed to big churches. We need churches of all sizes meeting the needs of different individuals. The first Sunday morning at Love Church we had 15 in the service. The average church in America has less than 150 people on any given Sunday morning. It is nice that our Love Church family has seen slow but steady growth over the years. The truth is reaching a certain attendance figure does not guarantee pastoral happiness. John 13:17 (KJV) says: *"If you know these things, happy are ye if you do them"* Happiness comes as a result of doing the right thing in the right way. I used to be jealous of a large area church with many busses. We purchased two church busses and they caused us nothing but headaches. I can honestly say that God had helped me not to be jealous of any other church ministry in town. I have learned from this failure and I am blessed for whomever God sends our way to our church family.

Failure # 12 – Believing a lie that I would be fulfilled in ministry if we were able to purchase a certain building.

Failure number 11 leads to failure number 12. Pastoral happiness cannot be achieved purchasing a certain building. Many years ago in our first church ministry we purchased a building that we couldn't afford to operate. We had to sell the building and move. Many church buildings are up for sale across our nation. We need to learn to be content with what we have until God gives another building.

Failure # 13 – Believing a lie that God made a serious mistake by calling me as a leader.

This failure is a very popular one among God's leaders. Moses thought God made a mistake in calling him. Jeremiah thought God made a mistake in calling him. The fact is that almost all leaders at one time or another thought God made a mistake in calling them into leadership. I am amazed that a perfect God has only imperfect people to use for His perfect plans. Pastor Bob Yawberg once said: "Only one out of ten pastors who start out in ministry cross the finish line." The truth is God knows our strengths and weaknesses. He knows what He is doing when He calls His leaders. People often change their minds and their opinions about their leaders. God doesn't change His mind. I just have to trust God that He knows what He's doing in calling me to leadership regardless of my feelings or circumstances.

Failure # 14 – Believing a lie that my church family was more important to God than lovingly leading my earthly family.

I've heard certain leaders say: "If you put your ministry first, God will take care of your families for you." In our first church ministry I believed that lie with serious consequences. We had church activities almost every night of the week. We had little family time and I was the reason. I learned a hard lesson to put my family first and my church family second. I cannot lead without a strong marriage and a strong family. God raised up the family first and the church second. I asked my daughter a question when she was younger. "Mary Ann – do you believe your daddy loves you and our family more or does he love Love Church more?" She said "Our family." I was blessed because I learned from the failure of misplaced priorities and I thank God for it.

Failure # 15 – Believing a lie that I didn't need Christians from other church families.

I come from an "independent" background. Our denominational churches put that non-Biblical word on our church signs and we were proud of it. It can be good to be independent in the sense that we don't have anyone outside of our church family to tell us what to do. Practically, however, it means we don't need other Christians from other church families. The Apostle Paul tells us in the 12th chapter of First Corinthians that we need every part of Christ's body. Ephesians chapter four tells us that part of Christ's body supplies something that we all need from one another. Independence can turn into isolation very easily. Satan loves to pick off one believer or one church family at a time. In my opinion, no church family has been more blessed and encouraged by building relationships with other church families than Love Church.

Failure # 16 – Believing a lie that other Christians and other church families were my competitors rather than future friends and allies.

Failure number fifteen leads to failure number sixteen. I was raised in the fundamental church to believe that all the other churches were wrong and we were right. It was OK to sheep-steal and bad-mouth any other church family. We had a neighboring church family that tried to bribe our people away to attend their church family with food and prizes. One pastor told me: "If you can get people away from another church, do it." The truth is 75% of our town didn't attend church services anywhere last Sunday. Many churches are growing because they have learned how to put on a better show and attract people away from other church families. I don't believe that is real growth. I believe our Lord is offended when God's people see themselves as competitors rather than as precious members of His Body-The Church. The truth is no one local church family will meet every spiritual need in town. God raises up specific church families to reach specific needs. Thank God for His Church.

Failure # 17 – Believing a lie that the death, burial and resurrection of Jesus Christ for one's personal salvation is not the total basis for Biblical based Christian unity and ministry partnership.

I Corinthians 15:1-3 tells us that the gospel is the death, burial and resurrection of Jesus Christ. Romans chapter six repeats this same truth. Romans 10:9-10 tells us that anyone who believes in the death, burial and resurrection in their heart and confesses that Jesus is Lord with their mouth shall be saved. People often ask me how I can work with certain religious groups. I can work with any group based on the true message of the gospel. Our fellowship is not based on the second coming, church rules or man's traditions. There is no true basis for working together apart from the gospel. Unfortunately many churches have allowed minor differences to hinder church unity and co-operation. Jesus prayed in John chapter 17 that His people would be one. I have made many mistakes in my ministry over the years. I have committed my life and ministry to see the prayer of Jesus for true unity to be demonstrated by God's people.

Failure # 18 – Believing a lie that our church family was "it" and other church families were inferior to our group.

In Luke 18:11 – we read about the Pharisee who prayed to himself with these words: *"God, I thank You that I am not like other people."* I tell our people, who are struggling with different forms of addiction, that I am also in the process of recovering. I am recovering from being a Pharisee. The Pharisees in the days of Jesus were proud of their religious accomplishments. They knew their Bible, never missed worship services, fasted, tithed and even gave money to the poor. The problem was they felt superior to

94

others. For many years I would not get together with other church families because I felt our church was superior to others. Thank God that I am being delivered daily from these prideful thoughts.

Failure # 19 – Believing a lie that I had to become like someone else to be successful in ministry.

I want to tell you about an imaginary friend that I have. His name is "Dr. Higgenlouper". He is the "expert" on all spiritual matters. All you have to do is attend one of his seminars and you can be an "expert" also. He can help you to have a big church in three weeks. He can explain all mysteries in the book of Revelation for only $59.95. He has all the answers for all needs. The only problem is that he doesn't exist except in my imagination. The truth is no one has all the answers. Paul said in Philippians 3:12 – *"Not that I have already obtained It, or have already become perfect, but I press on so that I may lay hold of that for which also I was laid hold of by Christ Jesus."* We need each other but we really can't walk a mile in someone else's' shoes. There is no one out there to fix us. We can't be someone else. We can never truly be successful by trying to be someone else.

Failure # 20 – Failure to believe that it was OK to be "me" as God made "me" in Christ.

A little boy who was the son of an actor was asked what his dad did for a living. He replied: "My dad's job is to be someone else." I am afraid there are a lot of pastors trying to be someone else. Dennis Kelley from Love Church tells me every week: "Be yourself, Pastor Phil." Paul warns in II Corinthians 10:12 about the danger of comparing yourself with someone else. I love Paul's testimony in I Corinthians 15:10 where he writes: *"But by the grace of God I am what I am…"* Being yourself doesn't mean you can't make changes to become more like Jesus. God always starts where we are on the way to becoming what we need to be. I have found there is great liberty in enjoying being who you are in

Christ. God is not looking for good actors. He wants to use the real "me".

Summary

The old hymn says God's grace is greater than all our sins. Luke 2:40 says that God's grace was upon Jesus. I used to think that God's grace was just for sinners who needed to be saved. Jesus didn't need to be saved but He needed God's grace to accomplish His mission on earth. We also need God's grace to overcome our failures and be all that God has designed us to be in Him. Fran and I work with a group of people plagued by failure and defeat. I thank God for my past failures, the present ones I am working on, and the future failures that I will experience. Romans 8:37 says: *"But in all these things we overwhelmingly conquer through Him who loved us."*

I have seen how God has used my family, my church background, my education, and even my failures to prepare me for inner-city ministry. Look back on your past and see what God has used to bring you to this place in your life. I am learning to truly rejoice and give God the glory for the difficult events in my life that are shaping me into the person I am becoming.

In Section III – we will examine God's faithfulness for inner-city ministry. I will share in Chapter 7 about God's faithfulness through our marriage of over 42 years. In Chapter 8, we'll see God's faithfulness through my military service. Chapter 9 deals with God's faithfulness through our 14 years at Fellowship Bible Church. Chapter 10 deals with God's faithfulness over the past 21 plus years at Love Church. I trust these pages are being used of God to examine your life and see how God can use you in greater ways.

SECTION III

GOD'S FAITHFULNESS FOR INNER-ITY MINISTRY

SCRIPTURES RELATING TO SECTION III

GOD'S FAITHFULNESS TO THE INNER-CITY

Deuteronomy 7:9 – *"Know therefore that the Lord your God, He is God, the faithful God, who keeps His covenant and His loving-kindness to a thousandth generation with those who love Him and keep His commandments."*

Isaiah 49:7 – *"Thus says the Lord, the Redeemer of Israel and its Holy One, to the despised One, To the One abhorred by the nation, to the Servant of rulers, kings will see and arise, princes will also bow down, because of the Lord who is faithful, the Holy One of Israel who has chosen You."*

Lamentations 3:22, 23 – *"The Lord's loving-kindnesses indeed never cease, for His compassions never fail. They are new every morning; Great is Your faithfulness."*

I Corinthians 1:9 – *"God is faithful, through whom you were called into fellowship with His Son, Jesus Christ our Lord."*

I Corinthians 10:13 – *"...God is faithful, who will not allow you to be tempted beyond what you are able, but with the temptation will provide the way of escape also, so that you will be able to endure it."*

I Thessalonians 5:24 – *"Faithful is He who calls you, and He also will bring it to pass."*

I John 1:9 – *"If we confess our sins, He is faithful and righteous to forgive us our sins and to cleanse us from all unrighteousness."*

CHAPTER 7

GOD'S FAITHFULNESS THROUGH THE MARRIAGE OF PHIL AND FRAN

SCRIPTURES RELATING TO CHAPTER 7

GOD'S FAITHFULNESS THROUGH THE MARRIAGE OF PHIL AND FRAN

Genesis 2:18 – *"Then the Lord God said, "It is not good for the man to be alone; I will make him a helper suitable for him."*

Genesis 2:24 – *"For this reason a man shall leave his father and his mother, and be joined to his wife; and they shall become one flesh."*

Proverbs 18:22 – *"He who finds a wife finds a good thing, and obtains favor from the Lord."*

Ecclesiastes 4:9, 10 – *"Two are better than one because they have a good return for their labor. For if either of them falls, the one will lift up his companion. But woe to the one who falls when there is not another to lift him up."*

Ecclesiastes 9:9 – *"Enjoy life with the woman whom you love all the days of your fleeting life which He has given to you under the sun, for this is your reward in life and in your toil in which you have labored under the sun."*

Matthew 19:6 – *"So they are no longer two, but one flesh. What therefore God has joined together let no man separate."*

I Corinthians 7:33 – *"But one who is married is concerned about the things of the world, how he may please his wife."*

Ephesians 5:21 – *"and be subject to one another in the fear of Christ."*

CHAPTER 7

GOD'S FAITHFULNESS THROUGH THE MARRIAGE OF PHIL AND FRAN

God's Word in Genesis 2:18 tells us that it is not good for a man to be alone. Adam had a perfect living environment. He walked with God everyday. He did not have to struggle with thoughts of sin and rebellion against God. All of his needs were met except for one. He was alone. God saw that he was alone and promised to make a helper suitable for him. He told Adam to take newly created Eve to be his wife and that they should be "one flesh" together.

King Solomon (who knew a lot about women) said that the person who finds a wife finds a good thing and obtains favor from the Lord. He further states in Ecclesiastes 4:9 that: *"Two are better than one…"* and tells his readers in Ecclesiastes 9:9 to: *"enjoy life with the woman whom you love all the days of your fleeting life…"* Jesus Himself said in Matthew 19:6 *"…what therefore God has joined together, let no man separate."* Paul says in Ephesians 5:21 that husbands and wives are *"…to be subject to one another in the fear of Christ."* Peter describes marriage partners in I Peter 3:7 as *"…a fellow heir of the grace on life…"* Marriage is important to God. He brought forth marriage and the family before he brought forth the church which bears His name.

Chapter 7 –"God's Faithfulness through the Marriage of Phil and Fran" is one of my favorite chapters in this book. It tells the story of two very different individuals who have been brought together by God to love each other, love their family and to love the poor and needy of the inner-city. Their marriage of 42 years is far from being perfect but it has given them a solid foundation from which to build and to learn to love. The truth is that a pastor does not have much of a public ministry unless he is learning to love and to be loved in his private ministry to his marriage and his family.

Let's look at this imperfect couple and see God's grace bringing it together and keeping it together over many challenges. Please remember to pray for your pastor that their marriage will truly be an example of God's love to others.

Marriage Background

I first met my future wife, Fran Case, when we were both young children attending the same conservative church family. I don't remember a lot about her except that she had red hair and was very shy. I had blond hair and I was not shy at all. Fran came from a Christian home and had two sisters and a brother. She was the oldest child and very responsible. Her father was a very hard worker working a variety of jobs in the local GMC plant. Her mother was an outgoing lady and a good stay-at-home mother. Her parents would later move out to Oakland Lake which I thought was a cool place to live. I can remember having singspirations after the evening service out at the Case home with the young people from our church. I believe I was eight years old when I first met Fran and she was about seven at the time. Fran loved to play the piano, fish the lake, and do bookkeeping all by herself. She never attended a football or basketball game at her high school. She was very good in class and never received a spanking in her life. She worked a job to help support her family and to buy her own car at the age of 16.

There is an old saying that says: "Opposites attract each other." I would have to agree that this saying was true in our life. I was not a good student; I received lots of spankings, enjoyed attending sports activities and loved crowds of people. I was a slob and Fran was not. She enjoyed being by herself and I enjoyed being with people. I was outgoing and Fran was shy. She was disciplined and I was undisciplined. I was loud and she was quiet.

Despite our tremendous differences, I believe God's faithfulness brought us together and has kept us together over many years. I sincerely believe that friendship is under-rated in marriage. Fran

102

has been my best friend over many years before and during our marriage. We both desire to bless each other. Lots of marriages have been shattered by a lack of friendship that keeps us going.

"Phil Mortensen Fan Club"

I know it sounds corny but I started the "Phil Mortensen fan club" when I moved from Pontiac, Michigan to Denver, Colorado. I wanted to find out how many girls would write to me after I moved 1,200 miles away at the age of 12. There was one girl who was faithful in writing and her name was Fran Case. I would come back to Pontiac during the summer break and I always looked forward to seeing Fran even though we both felt our relationship was "just friends". I will never forget when Fran was 15 she sent me a picture of herself. She wrote on the back of her picture that she believed in me and believed that I could accomplish what ever I set my mind and heart to do. It was a good feeling knowing that someone actually believed in me even though I thought of myself as a goof-off.

I moved back to Pontiac, Michigan at the age of 18 and stayed in the Case home on the back porch until I could find my own place. I will always be grateful to Fran's folks for providing a place for me to stay when I was "homeless". After getting my own apartment, Fran and I kept our friendship going. I would give her my opinion of the guys that she was dating. She would do the same for me in the girls that I was dating. I was dating a young lady and she told me that she wanted a black pearl ring. I was only making $39.99 a week in pay but I saved enough funds to purchase the ring. After I offered her the ring, she laughed at me and said she was only kidding. I went to Fran and she was very understanding of my painful situation. She was a good listener and I appreciated her friendship. I bought Fran the same type of ring several years later.

I began dating a girl from Detroit named Mary Martin whom I met at church camp. We got along well but there was 25 miles between us. I had an old car but it broke down many times. I had a date planned but I had no way to get to Mary's house. I asked Fran if she would drive me to Detroit and back. She took me on my date but she charged me $1.50 for gas. After the date was over; I kissed Mary good-night and Fran drove me home. That's what I call a true friend.

The longer I knew Fran the more I was blessed to be her friend. We even started dating for a while but I broke off the relationship on good terms because I wanted to give Fran freedom to date other guys and I wanted the freedom to date other girls. One day I felt impressed with these words: "Mortensen, Fran Case is a good woman. You better not let her go." I felt I needed to make her my wife despite my feelings of not being in love with her. I didn't know what love was at that time but I knew Fran was a good woman and a great friend.

"Will You Marry Me?"

I proposed at a church bowling league with these words: "Fran, I don't think I love you but I think I could learn to love you. Would you marry me?" Amazingly she accepted my proposal. People couldn't believe two such different people were actually getting married. I was 20 years old and Fran was 18.

Fran and I were scheduled to get married in the fall of 1965. Fran was planning a large wedding with beautiful fall colors. At the same time, Uncle Sam was making plans for me to be a part of his military service. I was scheduled to be drafted into the U.S. Army on July 12, 1965. I passed my army physical and was getting ready to do my duty. I found out about a rule that

104

married men were not to be drafted. On June 20, I shared with Fran that we would need to move our wedding date up to either July 3 or July 10 to avoid the military draft. Fran was disappointed with the change of wedding dates but she put the entire wedding together in less than three weeks. We were married in a beautiful ceremony with over 300 people in attendance on July 3, 1965. My Godly father performed the ceremony. Fran looked so beautiful and it was a very special day. Seeing Fran put that wedding together in three weeks showed me Fran's gift of administration and organization. Those gifts have been a wonderful blessing over the years. I was grateful to be married to my best friend and I was also grateful not having to be in the U.S. Army. God's faithfulness to us was to be shown in our marriage.

Marriage: The Early Years

Next to inviting Jesus Christ into my life and submitting to His personal Lordship in my life; the decision to marry Fran was the best one I've ever made. Neither Fran nor I knew totally what we were doing but we made a commitment that has lasted many years. The Apostle Paul said these words in II Timothy 1:12 (KJV): *"...I know whom I have believed, and am persuaded that he is able to keep that which I have committed unto Him against that day."* God is a God of commitment. Despite our human differences, Fran and I both love the Lord and we made a serious commitment to the Lord and to each other in sickness and in health, in good times and in bad times until death due us part.

That commitment would soon be tested. I was officially married ten seconds when Fran and I had our first time of "intense fellowship". Fran told me as were getting our pictures taken to get off her wedding dress. It's hard to fight in front of 300 people but I thought Fran wanted me to correct her. I was wrong. We later fought over how many wedding gifts we had to open at the reception. After a $65 four-day honeymoon, Fran and I began our married life together at 63 Norton Street, Apartment 5 in the inner-city of Pontiac, Michigan. The landlord charged us $20 a week

63 Norton St. Apt 5 (upper left)

including all utilities and cockroaches. We had to step over the drunks downstairs; but they were friendly drunks. Fran was not thrilled to be living in the inner-city to say the least. I found out the hard way that men and women think, feel and communicate differently. Eventually we moved twice before finding a nice house on Birchcrest Avenue with no cockroaches or drunks living below us. We thought we had moved to paradise. Our young marriage had survived nine months but a big change was about to happen which would change our lives and ministry forever. The government passed another new law that married men without children were to be drafted into the army. I was army bound, ready or not.

Our Marriage Following Military Service And Educational Training

I have written quite a bit about our marriage in Chapter 8 related to God's faithfulness through my military service. I also covered a lot about our marriage during my education preparations in Chapter 5. I don't desire to repeat myself so I want to jump ahead to 1974 following my graduation from Fort Wayne Bible College. I sincerely appreciated Fran's support during our four years of military service and four years of educational preparation. She worked outside the home overseas and in the United States. It wasn't easy putting our two year old son into day-care at 7:00 AM, but Fran did it to help me get my needed education. It wasn't easy for her to work outside the home, inside the home and also being a pastor's wife all at the same time; but Fran did it.

Trusting God

In September of 1974 I quit my job at the Veterans Hospital in Fort Wayne. I felt the Lord wanted me to trust Him for full-time financial support. Despite our fears, Fran supported me. I appreciated that support so much. I didn't have a clear vision as a pastor in those early days. I know now that God was faithful to Fran to help her trust Him when she couldn't fully trust her unstable husband. We would get depressed at times looking at other married couples who seemed to have perfect marriages. There were many times that we barely made it financially. I remember so clearly the month that we had to trade in extra pop bottles to pay our expenses. For eleven years we never passed the offering plate to pay our bills. We placed a simple box in the back and encouraged our people to honor the Lord in their tithes and offerings. God never let us down even though we let Him down many times.

I believe our life- style taught our son and our daughter to trust the Lord when we couldn't trust our feelings or our circumstances. I am so grateful that I have been able to maintain a diary since 1971. I have seen the faithfulness of God to meet our every need for many years. We have been so blessed to see God's faithfulness through hundreds of supportive friends over the years. I am so grateful that I yielded my life to be a pastor.

Marriage Through Many Ups and Downs

I agree completely with Fran's words when she said: "When we started Fellowship Bible Church, it was your ministry. When we started Love Church it has been our ministry." I know God called me to start our first work in the inner-city but my wife and family were not the priority they should have been. My attitude was church first, family second. We had some form of church activity going almost every night at Fellowship Bible Church. We rarely had family nights and I was not willing to live on a financial budget. My ego was built because I felt the people "needed me".

107

My family needed me more but I failed to see it at the time. I know God and my family has forgiven me but I just want to challenge any pastor who may have their priorities out of order. On a recent survey almost 90% of the wives of pastors questioned said they wished their husband had chosen some other occupation rather than being a pastor. Fran did her best to support me at Fellowship Bible Church but we were never truly ministry partners until God raised up Love Church in 1986.

A New Experience

We resigned under good circumstances from Fellowship Bible Church in late November of 1985. For the next year we experienced what many poor and needy people experience. We had to live on $15 a month from food stamps. I was out of work for several months and needed to attend government training sessions to survive. Several churches such as First Missionary Church and Broadway Christian Church provided food and financial support. We learned how to beg like the poor have to beg. My manhood took a terrible beating. I was depressed and felt discouraged that I wasn't providing for the financial needs of my family. I will always be grateful for Christians from many church families who helped us survive probably the most difficult year of our marriage and of our lives. I spent some time in the hospital and that experience gave me greater compassion for hospital patients. I even lost my father to death in 1986. I will never, ever conduct a funeral the same way after losing my father. God was faithful through our hurts, pains, poverty and challenges. It was rough but it was fruitful.

A New Direction

In the spring of 1986 I felt Fran and I were ready to start a new church plant called "Love Church". Fran did not feel the same way as I did. She was still hurting from the pains of being a neglected pastor's wife of 14 years at Fellowship Bible Church. We argued constantly about the timing of starting our new work. I will always remember the message on the answering machine from Fran. She said she would support me in starting the new work regardless of her feelings. I felt GREAT! I won the argument. I thought I would invite Pastor Bob and Marilyn Yawberg over to confirm my decision to start Love Church immediately.

Boy! Did they ever come over! Bob pointed his finger at me and said these words that I will never forget: "Phil, you and your wife are not ready to start a new church work." He gave me about five good reasons for his answer. I wanted to punch him but I knew in my spirit that he was correct. Every pastor needs a pastor who will be lovingly honest with them as they see it. I took Bob's counsel very seriously. I delayed starting Love Church for several months until Fran was totally behind my efforts. I even agreed to start our new church on Sunday and Wednesday evenings and attend Broadway Christian Church on Sunday mornings. This united decision gave our marriage time to heal. We were able to take in on Sunday mornings and give out on Sunday and Wednesday evenings. We started Love Church, united, together 21 years ago and we are still united, maintaining our priorities of family first and church second. Fran loves being a pastor's wife and being my wife. She does not have to compete with Love Church for my attention. We enjoy family nights off and at least three weeks of vacation together each year. We try to take a day off each week, but that is a challenge because of our many activities. We are together on the same page. Church life can tear a marriage apart. We are grateful that due to God's faithfulness, He has used the ministry of Love Church to bring us together. I thank God for Fran's support until I could get my priorities in order.

It has been a challenge pastoring a church focused on the needs of the poor and needy. It has taken much time and effort to build relationships with over 100 church families. It has been a challenge reaching out to our needy inner-city. We still find time for each other and for our children and eight grandchildren. The older we get the more physical challenges we face. We simply don't have the same degree of energy that we had 36 years ago when we started Fellowship Bible Church. Little did we know that the greatest challenge was yet to come.

A New Challenge

In the fall of 2004 Fran was told that she had colon cancer. She would need surgery and chemo treatments following her surgery. After extensive X-rays we were shocked by what the doctor found. Fran always took good care of her body. She ate the right foods and exercised faithfully. She does not come from a family with a history of cancer. The cancer was diagnosed as stage four, which is very serious. We don't understand why Fran has and is going through this very difficult experience. We do know that God is good and He is to be trusted when our feelings cannot be trusted.

Fran was faced with a choice to either give up in despair, or fight the good fight of faith. Thankfully she chose the latter. We have seen the faithfulness of God through very difficult circumstances. We have seen the kindness of God's people like Rachel Presser who sat with Fran through many chemo treatments. We have received wonderful encouragement from Nelda McNary, a pastor's wife, who fought cancer herself for the past ten years and done so with a joyful attitude. Fran has been blessed with the kindness shown to her by Pastor Jack Teeple. Pastor Jack has gone through cancer himself. He calls Fran regularly and prays with her on the phone. Many concerned people have brought over meals when Fran was too tired or too sick to prepare meals herself. One night we had Christians from over 20 different church families come and pray over Fran, including a number of pastor's wives. Thank God for family and friends who sincerely care about us. May our marriage always demonstrate God's faithfulness.

CHAPTER 8

GOD'S FAITHFULNESS THROUGH PHIL'S MILITARY SERVICE

SCRIPTURES RELATING TO CHAPTER 8

GOD'S FAITHFULNESS THROUGH
PHIL'S MILITARY SERVICE

II Timothy 2:3, 4 - *"Suffer hardship with me, as a good soldier of Christ Jesus. No soldier in active service entangles himself in the affairs of everyday life, so that he may please the one who enlisted him as a soldier."*

Matthew 8:8-10 – *"But the centurion said, "Lord, I am not worthy for You to come under my roof, but, just say the word, and my servant will be healed. For I also am a man under authority: with soldiers under me; and I say to this one, "Go!" and he goes to another, "Come!" and he comes, and to my slave, "Do this!" and he does it." Now when Jesus heard this, He marveled and said to those who were following, "truly I say to you, I have not found such great faith with anyone in Israel."*

Luke 3:14 – *" Some soldiers were questioning him, saying, "And what about us, what shall we do?" And he said to them, "Do not take money from anyone by force, or accuse anyone falsely, and be content with your wages."*

Matthew 27:54 – *"Now the centurion, and those who were with him keeping guard over Jesus, when they saw the earthquake and the things that were happening, became very frightened and said, "Truly this was the Son of God!"*

II Timothy 4:7 – *"I have fought the good fight, I have finished the course, I have kept the faith"*

I Corinthians 9:7 - : *Who at any time serves as a soldier at his own expense?"*

John 15:13 – *"Greater love has no one than this, that one lay down his life for his friends."*

112

CHAPTER 8

GOD'S FAITHFULNESS THROUGH PHIL'S MILITARY SERVICE

Military Service and the Bible

All through the Bible we see the importance of military service. God gave His people the Promise Land but He told them they would have to fight for it. The book of Joshua describes many military operations. Joshua was a great soldier as well as a great man of faith. He and Caleb were the two spies who trusted God to give them military victory over the giants in the land. Each man was expected to serve in the military with the exception of those who were in the first 12 months of married life. Samson was greatly used in military service against the Philistines. Gideon was chosen by God to defeat a mighty army with only 300 soldiers. David was a great military leader despite his faults. According to I Samuel 15:3, King Saul was removed from the throne by God for failing to follow God's orders to put to death every man, woman, child, infant and animal belonging to the enemy. Nehemiah 4:17-18 tells us how Nehemiah led a great effort to rebuild the walls of Jerusalem by instructing each man to have a tool in one hand and a weapon in the other hand. God even used the enemies of His people to put them into captivity for 70 years as a punishment for their disobedience against Him.

We see many references in the New Testament to military service. In the days of Jesus, Israel was occupied by the Roman army. The Roman soldiers were despised by the Jewish people for occupying their land. Despite these feelings of hostility Jesus often communicated with the Roman soldiers. He taught them in Luke 3:14 not to take any money by force or false accusation. He encouraged them to be content with the wages they were being paid. He told his followers to be willing to carry the military gear of the soldiers two miles even if they were only required to carry it one mile. He described the faith of a soldier in Matthew 8:8-10 as the greatest example of faith Jesus had found in Israel. A soldier acknowledged Jesus being the Son of God in Matthew 27:54.

Jesus described in John 15:13 the greatest example of love was for a person to lay down their life for another; something which soldiers were expected to do for one another. The Apostle Paul used the example of soldiers several times in his writings. In I Corinthians 9:7, he said soldiers should be paid. He challenged Timothy in II Timothy 2:3-4 to suffer hardship with him as a good soldier of Christ Jesus. He reminded Timothy that a soldier's first responsibility was to please the one who had chosen him to be a soldier. He warned him about the dangers of a soldier getting involved in the affairs of everyday life. God's Word describes His people as warriors, conquerors and part of His army. Jesus is beautifully described in Revelation 19:11-21 as seated on a white horse leading a military victory over all His enemies.

Military Service at Fort Leonard Wood, Missouri:

"I'm not a bolo – I'm not a bolo!"

In early 1966, Uncle Sam passed a new law requiring married men with no children to serve in the military. We had over 500,000 men and women serving in SouthVietnam and Uncle Sam needed more personnel. He did this by reaching out to me. I passed my military physical and was set to be drafted into the U.S. Army on Monday, March 21, 1966. I checked out several military options. I didn't want to be a Marine because they were crazy. I didn't want to join the Navy because I couldn't swim. I didn't want to join the Air Force because I didn't like to fly. The U.S. Army was the only other choice. I was told I would get better duty if I enlisted for four years rather than be drafted for two years. I was encouraged to go into military security and be a part of the military police. I was told by my recruiter that I would be investigating military crimes. He lied! I was told by my recruiter that after basic training I could live with my wife off post with my wife at Fort Gordon in Augusta, Georgia. He lied! On Friday March 18 at

114

5:23 PM I raised my right hand and joined the U.S. Army. I left Detroit, Michigan and headed for beautiful Fort Leonard Wood in Waynesville, Missouri. It was an experience that would change my life forever.

I got off the bus at Fort Leonard Wood and immediately some army sergeant started to yell at me. I soon learned two important lessons: One, I wasn't in charge of the organization that I had just joined and two, they were in charge and I was their military property. Most of the sergeants must have had problems with their hearing because they continually told me, "I can't hear you." We were housed in fairly new quarters comprised of three floors. We were given many opportunities to run up and down the stairs connecting those three floors when the sergeants didn't feel we were moving fast enough. My drill sergeant yelled at me for nine weeks. He yelled at me at 5:00 AM, thinking that would be an excellent time for my body to experience exercise like running around outside in chilly temperatures in my underwear. As a result, I experienced two bouts of pneumonia, ending up in the military hospital both times.

We had eight minutes to eat what the army called "Food". I had a good roommate named Steve and he helped me a lot to cope with military life. Several times I was able to call long distance to Fran at home in Michigan. Military life can be very lonely at times but I was doing OK –overall.

My hardest test was yet to come. I had never fired a weapon in my life. In order to graduate from basic training, you had to knock down at least 30 targets out of 84 targets from different distances and different positions. I missed several weeks of target practice when I was hospitalized. Our sergeant assured us that anyone who did not knock down at least 30 targets would be re-assigned and start basic training over until they completed this task. I did not want to fail. Those who did fail were called "bolos". Nobody wanted to be a "bolo", including me.

When the big day finally arrived – I knocked down 29 targets out of a possible 82 targets. This meant I had to knock down at least one target with two bullets left. I squeezed the trigger and by an act of Almighty God, my 30th target fell down. I yelled, "I'm not a bolo –I'm not a bolo."

Knocking down that 30th target was one of the greatest emotional moments of my life. I felt so good about myself. I was going to graduate from basic training on time with my proud family in attendance. I felt proud being a part of something much bigger than myself. I worked hard, looked my best and felt a real sense of accomplishment. My body and my mind were in the best shape of my life. It felt great to march across the parade grounds hearing applause from those in attendance. I was a proud solider in the United States Army.

Military Service at Fort Gordon, Georgia and in Warrenton, Virginia

My next stop was military police school at Fort Gordon, Georgia outside of Augusta. This was in the hot summer of 1966. I was looking forward to investigating military crimes following my graduation from Fort Gordon. Fran and I were looking forward to living off-post in Augusta. Fran found an apartment not far from the base. She also found hundreds of the biggest, meanest Georgia cockroaches God ever allowed to multiply. We were told that we could not live off post but perhaps we could see each other on the weekends. I was told to report for duty on a Sunday evening promptly at 6:00 PM. They would not even allow me to leave post to spend one final afternoon with Fran before she left for Michigan. I came up with a great idea. I  would simply get into the trunk of my car and sneak past the guards at the main gate. Fran went along with the plan, releasing

116

me from that hot trunk about a mile off-post. We had a nice afternoon together but it was soon time to return. I got back into the trunk and this time it was very hot and humid. It seemed like forever before Fran opened the trunk on-post where no one could see us. I kissed her good-bye and reported for duty by 6:00 PM. Military training at Fort Gordon wasn't bad except for the grueling heat and humidity. After graduating from military school, all 60 of us received our military orders. Fifty-eight men out of our unit were assigned to South Vietnam. Another man named Stuart and I were assigned to a small military post 40 miles outside of Washington D.C.; a place called Vent Hill Farms Station in Warrenton, Virginia.

Fran and I lived in a trailer outside of our army post in Warrenton. Fran worked several jobs to help with our family finances. I believe my monthly paycheck was less than $80. We did not have much money but we had each other and our marriage really began to grow. My favorite memory of the six months of military life in northern Virginia happened on Thanksgiving Day of 1966. We had a kitten and he was very playful. Fran made a beautiful turkey dinner with all the trimmings. Unfortunately the kitten got to the turkey before we did. After we threw out what was left of the turkey; we settled on hotdogs for Thanksgiving. I had 35 cents to my name and I bought my wife a piece of pumpkin pie for dessert. It was a Thanksgiving I will never forget and it brought us closer together.

Overall Fran and I really enjoyed our military stay in northern Virginia. Military duty was relatively easy. Our neighbors were kind. It was enjoyable attending a true, southern, country church. It was a strange experience for us seeing half of the people taking a smoke break between Sunday school and the Sunday morning service. We were taught early in life that you couldn't really love Jesus if you smoked a cigarette. Our smoking Christian friends at that rural church showed us a different reality. While stationed in northern Virginia I noticed a number of the men in my unit were being transferred to South Vietnam. I knew I could also be transferred to South Vietnam but I preferred to live in Germany

117

with my wife if the army would allow for this to happen. I put in for a transfer and was eventually sent to West Berlin, Germany in March of 1967.

Military Service in West Berlin, Germany
(March 1967-March 1970)

God really began to change our lives while we were living in West Berlin. Fran was able to join me in May of 1967. We lived off-post in a lovely German second floor apartment. We loved the city even though it was surrounded by an evil wall. Nearly 100 East Germans lost their lives attempting to escape into West Berlin. We really enjoyed the people and we made many new friends,

In March of 1967 I was stationed at Andrews Barracks. Fran worked at a garage where U.S. military personnel would take their personal vehicles to be fixed. We didn't own a television or a car but we were happy together. My job title in West Berlin was Protocol Clerk. Because I could type I was blessed to transfer out of the military police and work in administration. I had the privilege of working for the sergeant-major, the executive officer and the top officer, Colonel Smith. My job was to take care of their personal needs and to arrange accommodations and transportation for visiting personnel. I typed up forms and got coffee for my supervisors. I was treated very well and I put forth a good effort. Having a good attitude makes a big difference.

"Mortensen - I thought you were a Christian."

My saddest memory of my military experience in West Berlin dealt with my attempt to witness to the executive officer who was also a major in the U.S. Army. I had an army New Testament on my desk. The executive officer and I became friends and I told him what Jesus Christ had done in my life. I invited him to make Jesus Christ his personal Savior and Lord. He seemed to be truly interested in what I had to say.

One of my jobs was making sure each of the three top men that I served received their mail on a daily basis. One day I went to get the mail and I noticed a popular men's magazine from Chicago showing nude women inside its cover. I looked around to make sure that no one was looking. I felt very confident that I could look inside the magazine and put it back inside the brown cover before my officer friend found out. As I was looking at its pages, I heard the following words that I will never forget: "Mortensen – I thought you were a Christian." He smiled at me as I returned his mail to him. I did not get into trouble but I was never able to talk to him about true spiritual matters again. I know the Lord has forgiven me but I learned a vital lesson. It is that our lives always speak so much louder than our words ever will.

Fran and I began to take an active part in the worship services at McNair Barracks Chapel in West Berlin located about two miles from Andrews Barracks. In the three years we attended these inter-denominational services God blessed us with two wonderful U.S. Army Chaplains – Chaplain Andrews and Chaplain Thompson.

We noticed there was no Sunday evening service or evening Bible study at McNair Barracks Chapel. In the summer of 1967, I requested permission from Chaplain Andrews to lead a Sunday night service. He gave me his blessing and his permission. The first Sunday night service we had six in attendance. Our piano player was a wonderful British Christian by the name of Mr. Darby Mr. Darby earned his living as a Berlin taxi driver. Leading the Sunday night services gave Fran and me an opportunity to work together in ministry. I am blessed to say that over 40 years later we all still working together in ministry. We will always be grateful for our ministry experience that started while serving in the U.S. Army. We began to see lives changed by God's power even though I was refusing the call of God on my life to be a pastor.

"Mrs. Mortensen that's the BEST "Kool-Aid" I have ever drunk in my life."

My wife Fran always felt sorry for what the GI's had to eat in the mess hall. Nothing ministers more to a soldier away from home than good, home-made cooking. Fran suggested she make a great Thanksgiving meal with all the trimmings. She got up at 2:00 AM to prepare a delicious traditional meal. We had mashed potatoes, gravy, vegetables, stuffing, rolls and a great dessert. The highlight was a delicious turkey, cooked to perfection. We invited six to eight GI's from our chapel services. They ate everything in sight. I asked the men what they thought of the meal. One GI replied, "Mrs. Mortensen that is the best "Kool-Aid" I have ever drunk in my life." Fran was greatly used of God to minister to many lonely men in the service. She also had an opportunity to take several Bible study correspondence courses which proved to be a great blessing to her.

On Wednesday, February 26 at 2:10 AM Fran and I became the proud parents of Michael David Mortensen who was born in the U.S. Army Hospital in West Berlin, Germany. Our total hospital bill cost us a total of $7.50. He turned out to be worth every cent of it. Our new son gave us the opportunity to work together even closer. Michael was a good baby and a great blessing to Fran and me.

"Phil how many people have you won to the Lord lately with your methods?"

We had a group of young people from Campus Crusade for Christ who came to Berlin in the spring of 1969. They shared the "Four Spiritual Laws" with everyone. They witnessed to GI's; to Communist students at the Free University, and to everyone else that was breathing. I watched them very closely and got convicted that I wasn't doing more to share my faith with others.

On Sunday, May 11, 1969 I was talking with Doug from Campus Crusade about the "inferior" witnessing techniques that I saw used by these sincere young people. I had the "gift of criticism" and my "ministry" was correcting those attempting to serve the Lord and share the gospel. After complaining to Doug, he asked me a question that changed my life, "Phil how many people have you won to the Lord lately with your methods?" I had no answer for Doug. Coming from my background, I loved to debate other Christians and point out their faults. After Doug's question, I felt a great sense of conviction from the Lord. I was determined to share my faith if God gave me the opportunity. The opportunity would arrive seven days later to share my faith on May 18, 1969.

The U.S. Army sponsored field trips to various points of interest in Berlin. On this particular Sunday we were scheduled to visit a place called Peacock Island. This area featured some beautiful peacocks. I was sitting on the bus and I noticed a lonely GI with a disfigured face named Herman. I felt drawn to him by the Spirit of God. God was about to do a great miracle of grace for both of us on that very special Sunday afternoon.

I asked Herman about his background. He was from a very rough section of New York City. His father died of alcohol abuse. His mother died of cancer. His sister was beaten up and killed by a gang. Her remains were thrown into the East River. Herman had been wounded while serving in South Vietnam. We talked about God and His love for us. Herman had never seen the inside of a Bible in his life. I shared the plan of salvation with him. I asked him if he would like to ask Jesus to come into his life. With tears in his eyes, he accepted Jesus Christ into his life with a simple, child-like prayer.

I was struggling in my own life with the call of God on my life to be a pastor. I saw the many struggles my beloved father endured as a pastor and I wanted nothing to do with the pastorate. The moment Herman invited Jesus into his life was one of the happiest moments of my life. I looked at the clock and it was 5:23 PM. I bowed my head and with tears I told God I would do anything He wanted me to do, including being a preacher. My life has never been the same since. I'm overwhelmed with the idea of introducing needy people to Jesus. He's the only One who can change their life from the inside and the outside. I was amazed that God was willing to use me to help people in this life and in the next and still make a living for my family. I was willing to study to be a pastor for Jesus but I didn't think any Bible college would accept me.

The Final Thirteen Months

The last 13 months of active duty in the U.S. Army were the most enjoyable and most productive. We were blessed with a healthy baby boy in Michael David. I earned the rank of Specialist E-5 (similar to buck sergeant) and we were able to move into nicely furnished government housing off-post. Fran's father Ed Case and her brother Bill were able to visit us in 1969. My parents and my sister Mari Joy were also able to visit us in 1969. It was a special blessing to see family in Berlin because we hadn't visited in the United States for three years.

Fran, Michael and I met my folks and my sister in Frankfurt, West Germany in August of 1969. We took a train to the French coast and crossed the English Channel docking in Great Britain. We were able to visit some sites in London before boarding a ship bound for West Germany. We rented a car and journeyed to Denmark where my father was born in 1913. My father was born in a small Danish village named Svinning; leaving his home in 1919 at the age of six. Fifty years later we stood in the very house where he was born. It was a real thrill.

Back in Berlin we had a change in command from one good man to another good man. Colonel Smith was replaced by Colonel Hamilton. We became very good friends. He would call me down into his office and recall Christian songs that he remembered as a boy growing up in church

I'll never forget when Colonel Hamilton visited our Sunday night service at McNair Barracks Chapel. Our son Michael was about six months old. Colonel Hamilton was wearing his beautiful dress blue uniform, freshly pressed. He asked me if he could hold our son in his arms. I told him yes. He picked up Michael and our son threw up all over his beautiful dress blue uniform. We were very embarrassed but Colonel Hamilton was a very understanding. Thank God!

I preached my very first sermon on the last Sunday night of 1968. We later saw a number of GI's come to know Christ through our efforts in the military chapel in Berlin. Average attendance grew from six to about sixty. We made many long lasting friendships. On Labor Day weekend of 1969, I introduced myself to a man named John Wimmel. We took him home for lunch. The friendship is still going today.

A number of soldiers with whom I developed a relationship are still going on today. A number of these soldiers later came to Fort Wayne and attended Fort Wayne Bible College. Several of these men are still in the ministry today. We had some good Bible studies and many men really grew in their faith as a result. The biggest challenge was seeing men leave our unit. Many of them ended up in South Vietnam. Many paid the ultimate price with their lives.

Specialist 5 Mortensen at his Army Desk

On Sunday night, March 8, 1970 I preached my last sermon at McNair Barracks Chapel in West Berlin. I was blessed as three servicemen gave their life to Jesus Christ, including a young man from Silver Springs, Maryland who continues to be our friend after almost 40 years. We really grew in our spiritual life during our time of serving the Lord and the soldiers who attended McNair Barracks Chapel.

On Wednesday, March 11, 1970 one year old Michael plus his mother and dad left Berlin for New York City and my honorable discharge from active duty that was to occur the next day. In many ways, it was a very sad departure from Berlin. We had not been in the United States together for almost three years. God used Berlin and our experience in the U.S .Army to demonstrate His faithfulness as we were willing to be used for His service. At 4:01 PM Thursday, March 12, I saluted a female officer and was officially released from active duty. It was a real privilege to serve the Lord in the U.S. Army. Fran and I were privileged to visit 12 countries in Europe during our three-year stay. We were blessed to meet many Christians including Phil and Joan Munnig, who served the Lord through Child Evangelism Fellowship in West Berlin. We still have contact with a number of friendships that were made during my military service.

I have learned more about Christ-like unity in the U. S. military chapels than I ever did from my church experiences as a child and young adult. I learned that sincere Christians can worship God regardless of race, creed or class. I learned the importance of building relationships across various church lines that I am still practicing today. In the army I really started to learn to appreciate my wife, Fran, as my best friend and ministry partner. The most important thing I've learned is that God is a faithful God. He will guide and provide as we yield our lives to Him; including serving in the inner-city. In Chapter 9 let's see how God has shown His faithfulness to Phil and Fran in their ministry from 1971 to 1985 at Fellowship Bible Church.

CHAPTER 9

GOD'S FAITHFULNESS THROUGH
FELLOWSHIP BIBLE CHURCH-FORT WAYNE

GOD'S FAITHFULNESS THROUGH
FELLOWSHIP BIBLE CHURCH-FORT WAYNE

I John 1:3 - *"What we have seen and heard we proclaim to you also, so that you to may have fellowship with us; and indeed our fellowship is with the Father and with His Son Jesus Christ."*

I John 1:7 - *"but if we walk in the Light as He Himself is in the Light, we have fellowship with one another, and the blood of Jesus His Son cleanses us from all sin."*

II Corinthians 2:14 - *"But thanks be to God, who always leads us in His triumph in Christ, and manifests through us the sweet aroma of the knowledge of Him in every place."*

I Samuel 22:1, 2 - *"So David departed from there and escaped to the cave of Adullam; and when his brothers and all his father's household heard of it, they went down there to him. Everyone who was in distress, and everyone who was in debt, and everyone who was discontented gathered to him; and he became captain over them. Now there were about four hundred men with him."*

Matthew 9:27 - *"As Jesus went on from there, two blind men followed Him, crying out, "Have mercy on us, Son of David!"*

Galatians 2:9, 10 - *"and recognizing the grace that had been given to me, James and Cephas and John, who were reputed to be pillars, gave to me and Barnabas the right hand of fellowship, so that we might go to the Gentiles and they to the circumcised. They only asked us to remember the poor the very thing I also was eager to do."*

CHAPTER 9

GOD'S FAITHFULNESS THROUGH FELLOWSHIP BIBLE CHURCH-FORT WAYNE

God's Desire for Fellowship

The Bible tells us that our God is a God who desires fellowship with His creation. I John 1:3 tells us that our fellowship as Christians is with our Heavenly Father and His Son, Jesus Christ. God not only wants us to have fellowship with Him but fellowship with each other according to I John 1:7. David was a man described as a man with a "heart after God". Despite many faults and shortcomings, he was greatly used of God. Jesus was known as the "Son of David". We read in I Samuel 22:1-2 that David attracted a group of 400 men with serious needs. David could relate to the common man. As a young man He served the Lord as a humble shepherd. Paul tells us in Romans 12:16 to *"...associate with the lowly."*

God raised up the Church headed by His Son Jesus Christ to have fellowship with God's people. Acts 20:28 tells us that Jesus purchased the Church with His own blood. I Corinthians 3:17 tells us that God would destroy anyone attempting to destroy God's temple which is His people. Paul rejoiced that the right hand of fellowship was offered to him and Barnabas in Galatians 2:9-10 along with the charge to help the poor which Paul was eager to do.

The next few pages tell us of God's faithfulness upon the ministry of Fellowship Bible Church in Fort Wayne, Indiana from 1971 until 1985. It is impossible to list everything that happened at Fellowship Bible Church during these 14 years. The next few pages will summarize the highlights for each year including the church verse for the year plus quotes and key events. II Timothy 2:13 tells us that God is faithful regardless of the actions of His people. It is my hope that the reader may learn afresh of God's faithfulness.

127

1971

"...From everyone who has been given much, much will be required..." Luke 12:48 –

Events to Remember and Quotes to Ponder

- During the 1970 – 1971 school years at Fort Wayne Bible College, I had the privilege of singing with "The Redeemed Quartet" comprised of Dave Keefer, Keith VanTilberg, Gene Baker and myself. This ministry gave us the opportunity to visit many different churches of different sizes.

- Jim Clifford was a blessing to me in the area of personal evangelism and outreach.

- On June 17 God showed me Genesis 39:2 where He prospered Joseph through a variety of challenges. I believed God would prosper us if we were obedient to start Fellowship Bible Church. God opened a storefront building for us at 2707 South Calhoun that we rented for $125 per month including all utilities. Fort Wayne Bible College gave their blessing to allow students to attend Fellowship Bible Church.

- Sunday, December 5, 1971 was a day I will never forget. It was the first day of services for Fellowship Bible Church. We had 21 in Sunday School, 28 in the morning service and 20 in the evening service. I preached on the subject, "Guidelines for Christian Fellowship" from I John 1:3, our church verse.

- We passed out prayer request slips and someone requested prayer for their alcoholic husband. It shocked me that God would send people to us with real needs on our first Sunday. It was a preview of things to come. Several weeks later we went Christmas caroling in the inner-city. We found a lady in her home who told us she was thinking of killing herself. She said our songs gave her hope. She and her husband later became faithful members. On Sunday evening, December 26, God gave me the opportunity to preach to just one man sitting on one of our nine old wooden pews. Fran had to take our son to the nursery and I preached to Harold Stabler. I felt like telling him to go home. God gave me an internal word. He said, "If you won't be faithful in preaching to one; I'll never use you to preach to 100." It was one of the most important lessons God has ever taught me on faithfulness. We made a lot of mistakes starting Fellowship Bible Church but God was faithful to us then as He still is today.

1972

I Samuel 15:22 "...to obey is better than sacrifice..."

Events to remember and quotes to Ponder

- On Wednesday night, January 12, while working for a local dairy store, Gordy Croker and I were robbed at gunpoint. It was pretty scary looking at a pistol pointed straight at me. The robbers were later captured but it did give me a greater appreciation for many inner-city residents who live with the fear of crime on a daily basis.

- Several weeks later someone failed to lock the back door of the church, allowing the 24 below zero winter air to come inside. As a result Fran played the piano in 35 degree temperature inside our building. The next Sunday morning January 30, 1972 we dedicated our humble facility and ministry to the Lord. Pastor Paul E. Paino was our dedication speaker. He said these words that I will never forget, "As long as the doors of this facility are open, Satan cannot do what he wants to do in this neighborhood." Those words are still a great source of encouragement nearly 36 years later.

"Pastor Phil, our church building is on fire!"

131

- A major challenge happened to us on May 12. We gathered several hundred people from various churches for a Jesus walk against drug abuse. We walked over 20 miles in cold, wet weather. We had a praise rally at the Bible College that evening. At about 8:30PM that evening, I received a phone call from Grandma Lee. She said, "I have bad news for you Pastor Phil. Our church building is on fire." I went over to our humble facility to see it engulfed in flames. After the fire we lost a lot of people who began to doubt our ministry. Simpson United Methodist Church was kind enough to allow us to use their facility on Sunday afternoons. We held services in five different facilities in 1972. God was giving us the opportunity to be faithful through different trials. Once again it gave me a greater understanding of many urban residents who constantly move.

- We were able to purchase a humble house located at 120 W. Pontiac. This later became a great source of ministry for the homeless. We saw a number of people come to know the Lord and follow the Lord in baptism in 1972. We had a record attendance of 61.

1973

Ephesians 3:20 "Now to Him who is able to do far more abundantly beyond all that we ask or think, according to the power that works within us."

Events to Remember and quotes to Ponder

- We began the New Year checking out the possibility of buying our first home. We found a four-bedroom home located seven blocks from Fort Wayne Bible College at 1148 Kinnaird Avenue. We offered $13,900 which was less than the owner wanted. We waited patiently for the next six months while God worked out all the details. We were finally able to purchase our home for our price on July 3, 1973, our eighth wedding anniversary. It's a blessing to mow your own grass. I would love to see more inner-city residents be able to own their own home. Many of these needy people have never had the privilege of owning their own home. They have not been able to get bank loans due to unfair laws or racial prejudice. Scam artists prey on these individuals with empty promises and high interest rates which fosters further despair and hopelessness.

- We spent the entire year trying to survive in a rented facility located on South Lafayette. Our church facility had more mice in it than church members. Three times during the winter we had no heat for our services. God gave us some faithful workers despite our facility.

- On May 27, 1973 I was ordained by the Marimont Church. This is the church that my dad pastored for seven good years between 1951 and 1958. I thank God for the 22 years of ministry and fellowship which that church family provided. I am also grateful for a Bible-based foundation they provided. Jesus had a dove fly over His head on His

ordination. I had a sparrow fly over my head on my
ordination. It swooped down out of the church attic.

- I spent the summer of 1973 working at the Veterans
  Hospital in Fort Wayne. I completed three years of college
  life with one more year to go. We were able to put a
  church constitution into place along with a new elder and
  deacon board. We celebrated our second church
  anniversary thanking the Lord.

1974

Joshua 24:15 "...as for me and my house, we will serve the Lord."

Events to Remember and Quotes to Ponder

- Nineteen seventy-four was an important year for the Mortensen family and the ministry of Fellowship Bible Church. I was in my last semester at Fort Wayne Bible College. I placed seventh out of fifty-three students who took the Senior Bible Exam. On Sunday, May 5, I graduated from Fort Wayne Bible College with a 2.65 grade point average. I am grateful at everyone at Fort Wayne Bible College that helped me receive a quality education.

- We produced our first church newsletter entitled "Inner-City Insights". Our church family was able to move from our terrible facility on Lafayette Street to much nicer facilities at 2707 S Calhoun –right across the street from where we started in 1971. We were used of God to help Bible College students learn to apply their book learning to real life needs. We developed relationships with many students. We are still friends with them, years later.

- I was hired again to work at the Veterans Hospital. We put on a vacation Bible School averaging over 60 kids per night. Our dear friends, Pastor Harold and Janice Gingerich, put on special meetings for us in July. In August of 1974 I was challenged by our people to trust God for full-time employment with Fellowship Bible Church. I wanted to serve God full-time but I was afraid to trust Him. I went into the men's room of the hospital and I asked God a question. "God, if I trust you for a full-time salary, will you let me down?" I heard a small voice inside me answer, "Son, what do you think?" It was the only answer I needed to hear. With Fran's blessings I trusted God for a full-time

135

salary for the next 11 years. I developed a relationship with Pastor Bob Yawberg and some other good pastors that was centered on prayer. We are still friends and we are still praying together today. Our rented building was sold and we moved to the third floor of Central Catholic High School which worked out great.

II Timothy 2:2 "The things which you have heard from me in the presence of many witnesses, entrust these to faithful men who will be able to teach others also."

Events to Remember and quotes to Ponder

- We were blessed to start the new year at Central Catholic High School which was our home for 18 good months. They treated us very well and I learned to appreciate their heritage even though it was very different from mine.

- We were blessed to work with individuals from the state school for mentally challenged adults. They were a great blessing. Every church family should have these dear people to be a part of their church family.

- I was privileged to hold special services for two weeks in Rohrsville, Maryland.

- God blessed our worship team with both a piano and organ.

- We saw steady growth at the school despite having to walk up 42 stairs to get to our worship facility. My mother paid a visit to our facility and she was very impressed with the love shown by our people.

- We had several people baptized into Christ including a former stripper, who had experienced seven bad marriages. We conducted six Bible studies which brought some depth to our numerical growth.

- We made contact with the leaders of First Church of God. They were attempting to sell their church building and two surrounding houses for $65,000. We didn't have a penny for the project but we made a verbal offer pending on God's faithfulness to help us raise the needed funds. One of our mentally challenged ladies gave the first dollar for the building fund. I wrote to 279 churches requesting funds to purchase the First Church of God facility. The problem was I had not built many relationships and little money was sent in as a result. I learned an important lesson. Build relationships first; then ask for the needed funds. We ended 1975 with $3.95 left in the general fund. Praise God!

II Peter 3:9 "The Lord is not slow about His promise, as some count slowness, but is patient toward you, not wishing for any to perish but for all to come to repentance."

Events to Remember and Quotes to Ponder

- Nineteen seventy-six was another vital year for Fellowship Bible Church and our family. We received word in January that Fran was expecting our second child in July. During the year we reached a total of 100 people on one Sunday morning. It took us over four years to finally reach the 100 mark. I write this to encourage pastors to be faithful while trusting God to bring the increase.

- Our building fund was coming along but we still needed about $5,000 additional for the down payment on the property we wanted to purchase. This property was on the corner of Piqua and East Wildwood. We had a stranger knock on our door who said God told him to come over and give us a check for the down payment. Fran opened the check and it was for $2,500. A couple of days later someone else put a check for $2,500 into our inside mail box. We had the funds for the down payment to purchase our facility. On April 11, 1976 we held a Jesus parade. We walked the one mile from Central Catholic High School to our new 3039 Piqua location. We had high attendance at all three services at our new location. There was a deep sense of God's presence, provision and goodness to us.

- On Sunday, April 25, Pastor Paul E. Paino along with Dr. Tim Warner, president of Fort Wayne Bible College helped to dedicate our new facility. It was a great day of celebration.

- On Wednesday, July 28, Fran gave birth to a beautiful healthy girl named Mary Ann. She was born at the Old

Lutheran Hospital. Four days later Fran played the piano at Fellowship Bible Church and didn't miss a Sunday service.

- Here's Life Seminar brought Fort Wayne Christians together for evangelism and unity.

- Fellowship Bible Church celebrated many trials during these five years but God was very faithful to us.

<u>1977</u>

No specific church verse

Events to Remember and Quotes to Ponder

- Nineteen seventy-seven turned out to be a very challenging year for our ministry. Fran and I began the New Year in Florida with our family. On our return we experienced wind chill temperatures in excess of 60 below zero.

- My prayer request in my diary for February 19 was to be more secure in God's love for me. My insecurity would play a major role in how I handled or mishandled some major upcoming events which would affect my home and church ministry.

- Our former assistant pastor called and said we were in trouble. He said a number of our leaders did not have confidence in my leadership and wanted to meet with us. I called a meeting for four o'clock on a Sunday afternoon. I found out later that the assistant pastor tried to get me fired while I was in Florida. I asked each of the elders and deacons to tell me publicly who they felt should the pastor-me or my assistant pastor. I was willing to step down if they felt the assistant pastor should be the main leader. Every man around the table with the exception of the assistant pastor said they felt Phil Mortensen was to be the main leader. The assistant pastor quit and took about 20 people with him. He sent me a letter threatening to try and take half of the property. The split was used of God to help me be a better leader. God taught me not to recruit people for selfish reasons like I recruited the former assistant pastor years earlier. I simply reaped what I sowed.

- Overall I felt I handled the situation pretty well but I still struggled with a lack of confidence in God and in my lack of leadership. We had our ups and downs for the rest of the year. We enjoyed our church building but it I did not stop having problems. Our former worship leader Norman Jones stole $400 from us his way out of town.

- I shed some tears on our sixth anniversary while I was reviewing God's faithfulness through a difficult year. Overall our financial giving increased and God was faithful to provide all of our needs.

1978

Psalms 84:11 "For the Lord God is a sun and shield; The Lord gives grace and glory; No good thing does He withhold from those who walk uprightly."

Events to Remember and Quotes to Ponder

- January 1978 was an amazing month for us and our ministry at Fellowship Bible Church. I was called to the burn unit of St Joe Hospital in Fort Wayne. a gas explosion caused a young mother and her two children from Fellowship Bible Church to be blown through a plate glass window. While the mother's hair was on fire; she rolled her 12 day old baby and her two year old son in the snow putting out the flames before putting out the flames on her own body. There were only two people allowed in the burn unit, the woman's husband and me, as her pastor. The event confirmed God's calling on my life as a pastor.

- Later that month we endured the "Blizzard of 1978" with 18 inches of blowing snow.

- My father retired from Moody in Chicago. I wanted him and mom to move to Fort Wayne but they felt the need to remain in Wheaton, Illinois.

- I learned a vital lesson on forgiveness. I kept the letter from the former assistant pastor who threatened us with legal action in 1977. God told me to burn the letter and reach out to my former assistant pastor as a friend. We did make it right with each other after I obeyed God and burned the letter.

- I fired one of my deacons and my nursery supervisor so they both could work on their terrible marriage. They eventually got divorced and left Fellowship Bible Church, but I knew it was the right thing to do to help them try to

143

salvage their marriage. I am still friends with them 30 years later.

- We continued to add people and we had some great times of worship together. Pastor Bob Richardson came from Pontiac, Michigan, and he was a great blessing, teaching on discipleship.

- We brought 16 churches together for a tent crusade which was a great blessing.

- The biggest challenge was financially maintaining our building with huge utility bills. Overall 1978 was a great learning year and I'm reaping the benefits yet today.

<u>1979</u>

Colossians 1:28 "we proclaim Him, admonishing every man and teaching every man with all wisdom, so that we may present every man complete in Christ."

Events to Remember and Quotes to Ponder

- January 1979 was the beginning of the slow decline of our ministry at Fellowship Bible Church which ended with my resignation as pastor in November of 1985. I share these experiences so that others in ministry can profit from them. I also share them because they were a great learning experience for our future ministry at Love Church. God was faithful regardless of the ups and downs of our ministry.

- Things at Fellowship Bible Church seemed to be going well. Sunday morning attendance was averaging around 175. Our leadership was being developed and church finances were growing as well. My greatest struggle was trying to be a people-pleaser. My two closest chosen advisors were my biggest critics. I could never please them no matter how hard I tried. I started to lose my joy and become more like them. I have no one to blame but myself and my insecurities.

- There was interest in becoming formally connected with a group of Christians in Chicago who had a major emphasis on discipleship. I selfishly believed I could save my position as head pastor by hiding behind the covering which they offered. On April 13, 1979, I entered into formal covenant with Don Wilson and his Chicago area church. It would be a ministry-changing direction with very serious ministry consequences for me, my family and Fellowship Bible Church. The group from Chicago had a strong emphasis on men being the leader in their family. Over-all it was a good emphasis but we had men who

145

didn't know the difference between being the leader of their family and being the dictator of it. It felt good initially to be a part of this group from Chicago.

- Due to financial stress, we signed a two-year contract to sell our church building and have Saturday night services.

- I wrote in my diary on November 14, 1979 that I was concerned that we were losing many inner-city people. I didn't realize at the time what a loss it would be.

1980

I John 3:16 "We know love by this, that He laid down His life for us; and we ought to lay down our lives for the brethren."

Events to Remember and Quotes to Ponder

- Nineteen eighty was a very difficult year for our ministry at Fellowship Bible Church. We continued to baptize a large group of new converts but something was missing. One of my house group leaders blew up at me. Much of his harsh words were justified. Our outreach emphasis began to fade. We turned our emphasis inward to ourselves.

- We started to have "in-house" controversies at Fellowship Bible Church. For instance, we had a serious controversy over the use of head covers for women from I Corinthians, chapter 11. We lost several people over it. The intention was good but the results were not. Fellowship Bible Church started out welcoming everyone. We drifted into two groups: "committed" which were the paper members and "non-committed" which were the non-paper members of our church. I turned into a legalist and lost much of my joy in Christ and the joy of being "me". We started to lose a lot of good people. We called them "covenant breakers." It is very painful to even write these words many years later. We demanded that the leaders, including the worship team, all dress up with ties around their neck. I refused to reach out to anyone who left our church family.

- We switched from Sunday morning worship to Saturday night worship at First Christian Church. They were very nice to us.

- I was switched from Don Wilson's leadership to being placed under Skip Anderson's leadership. Skip and his

147

wife Jill were good people and they really seemed to care about us.

- Our finances were coming in OK and I honestly couldn't see what I was doing wrong at the time. Some of our men took greater leadership in their families. We had less emphasis on the physical building and more emphasis on the people and that was a good thing. The bad things, however, outnumbered the good things. We lost inner-city people that we deeply loved because they couldn't "keep up" with the rest of us. The biggest loss was the loss of joy and me trying to be someone besides myself. I am so concerned years later to see other church families going the way of Fellowship Bible Church.

1981

II Timothy 2:3 "Suffer hardship with me, as a good soldier of Christ Jesus."

Events to Remember and Quotes to Ponder

- We had a major emphasis on what we called "public commitment". This is where an individual or couple would publicly pledge their loyalty to our leadership. It made me feel good to hear what these people publicly were saying, but it didn't last long in the majority of cases. My original intent in becoming involved with "covenant" and "discipleship," as taught by the Chicago Church group was very honorable. I wanted to see unstable people and unstable couples become stable in their relationship with Jesus Christ and with others. The problem is that only God can produce genuine stability and growth. Paul said in I Corinthians 3:6, *"I planted, Apollos watered, but **God was causing the growth."***(emphasis mine)

- We continued to develop our house groups that met during the week. The house groups gave people a chance to share. It also gave us a vehicle to develop leadership. Some of the house group leaders were real servants to the people. Some, unfortunately, were slave-drivers of the people. I'll never forget the day I had to "fire" one of my house group leaders. I had a terrible headache doing it but I felt like a real leader for the first time in a long time. I am still friends with that leader and I'm glad for the action I had to take at that time.

- We did have some good times. Our dear Jamaican friend Ansel Aiken led us in a series of special meetings which were well received.

- Our family took a great vacation to Glacier National Park and the West Coast.

149

- My father came and gave his blessing on the 10th anniversary of Fellowship Bible Church. That blessing was a real highlight of our ministry. We did enjoy more family nights and family time together.

- I became more involved in city-wide prayer efforts that are still bearing fruit 26 years later. Our church growth was stagnant with many more tests yet to come. I sincerely praise God for the experiences He allowed which make me a better man today.

1982

John 3:3 "Jesus answered and said to him, "Truly, truly, I say to you, unless one is born again he cannot see the kingdom of God."

Events to Remember and Quotes to Ponder

- We had a very "mixed bag" of ministry in 1982. We could get people to attend and give but the outreach under "covenant" and "discipleship" was difficult. The visitors didn't feel at home in our services. Several former disgruntled people who left Fellowship Bible Church tried to start their own churches but they all failed. It is much easier to criticize other imperfect leaders than to be a leader yourself.

- Out of the 107 people who made public commitment with us over a two and one-half year period twenty-nine were "covenant breakers" and left Fellowship Bible Church. Five people were very unstable with us Seventy-two were doing quite well with us at Fellowship Bible Church and one was properly released to another church. We went from a high of eighteen house groups to seven house groups with good people in all of them. We had house group leaders who were trying to help others with their problems but were having lots of unresolved issues themselves.

- I know God has forgiven me, but I wasn't the leader at home that God wanted me to be. Fran felt left out with her gifts and talents. I should have been more supportive. I caused Fran much pain and hurt which took years to heal. These events have given us a greater desire to see couples in ministry coming into all the blessings instead of simply being used of God.

- Through the trials God was faithful to us. We enjoyed wonderful teaching conferences at various sites.

- We were able to attract a good number of young couples leading to seven weddings in 1982.

- Pastor Bob Yawberg led a major effort bringing over 2,000 Christians together to close down X-rated book stores and X-rated movie theaters.

- I personally enjoyed working out at the local health club doing exercise and using the hot tub.

- We were blessed overall with a good group of Christians who were walking out stability and growth despite the ever declining numbers. Many days while fasting I sought the Lord for God's guidance and strength. Overall I was still grateful to be pastoring Fellowship Bible Church on our 11th anniversary.

1983

James 1:22 "But prove yourselves doers of the word, and not merely hearers who delude themselves."

Events to Remember and Quotes to Ponder

- Someone once said that the most important item on a person's grave marker is the dash in between a person's date of birth and the person' date of death. There are exciting times in ministry. There are down times in ministry. The real question is, "What are we doing with the dash mark days of our ministry?" Nineteen eighty-three was a dash mark year for Fellowship Bible Church. We didn't grow but we didn't lose either. We were basically maintaining our ministry. Unfortunately the majority of churches in the USA are simply maintaining their ministry year after year. Fellowship Bible Church lost a sense of urgency for outreach and we paid the price for many years.

- We experienced some positive events during the year. Some of our people were truly growing in the Lord. Church giving was going down but God was faithful to help meet our needs. We enjoyed good social times of softball, bowling and hay rides. We had 172 people in the church directory but I wasn't giving the real leadership Fellowship Bible Church that was needed.

- One of the most positive things I did personally was to begin to jog. I started with one lap around my alley going very slowly. After several weeks I was able to jog five times around the alley making one complete mile without stopping. Jogging helped to relieve the pressures produced from Fellowship Bible Church. I was able to finally run two miles. I even entered a two mile race and completed it. Eventually I was able to run six and two-tenths miles without stopping in 69 minutes.

- I spent some good times of private retreat at the humble Sedan Motel.

- Our family enjoyed visiting prisoners. This was something God has helped me do for almost 30 years.

- Acts 20:28 says, *"...Be on guard for yourselves and for all the flock..."* God helped me to build myself up with daily devotions, jogging, personal retreats and a good family vacation. I urge all pastors to build themselves up for ministry. You can't give out to others unless you are building yourself in all areas of life.

1984

Exodus 23:30 - "I will drive them out before you little by little, until you become fruitful and take possession of the land."

Events to Remember and Quotes to Ponder

- I was sincerely willing to resign as pastor of Fellowship Bible Church in 1984 but I felt God's call on my life to continue despite struggles and criticism. The great majority of my ministry challenges were self-inflected. I didn't believe I could lead effectively. I didn't believe I could hear from God for direction. The worst thing I did was to train my people to believe the same things about me that I believed about me. Pastor Skip from the Chicago church was a source of encouragement for me, but he couldn't lead for me.

- I heard about a downtown church building up for sale. It was a beautiful church building with high ceilings and lots of room for ministry. I asked the leadership of the downtown church if we could use the facility for one Sunday morning. They agreed. I can remember hearing the beautiful sound of the church bells ringing out before our Sunday mornings service. It was a great day. Several days later I met with a couple for breakfast in their home. Even though I didn't have a clear vision of ministry to the poor, I shared my excitement about the potential of that building being used to help poor people. After I shared my thoughts on future potential ministry to the poor, the husband looked at me and said these words, "Pastor Phil, that building was nice but I don't have any burden to help the poor and needy downtown." That was my first clue; I was in the wrong church. We didn't buy the building but I learned a lesson.

155

- On May 6 I completed my first marathon of 26 miles, 385 yards in the time of 5 hours, 7 minutes. There were actually seven runners slower than me and many didn't even complete the marathon. I was exhausted but I felt a real sense of accomplishment.

- Unity Lutheran School said that we could use their facility on Sunday morning and evening for a very reasonable rental price. God gave me an encouraging word that I was His "investment" and that still rings true today.

1985

Romans 15:1 "Now we who are strong ought to bear the weaknesses of those without strength and not just please ourselves."

Events to Remember and Quotes to Ponder

- A seasoned pastor once told me, "Phil in ministry, we don't deal with reality. We deal with people's perceptions of reality." There was a perception that things at Fellowship Bible Church were not going well. I remember reading in my diary the year before that 12 former Fellowship Bible Church men became pastors after they left us. One pastor who received some of our departing members told me they were the best servants in his new church. He told me they had been trained well in serving others under our leadership. If a person wears green sunglasses, everything appears green. If a person wears red sunglasses, everything appears red. If a pastor wears sunglasses of discouragement, everything appears discouraging. I was wearing those discouragement sunglasses.

- I was doing something right. I was getting closer to Fort Wayne area pastors who provided a real source of encouragement to Fran and me. The social times of recreation and trips temporally took our minds off of our ministry trials. I even completed my second marathon on May 5. I finished in the time of 4 hours 59 minutes improving on last year's time by 18 minutes.

- Fran and I went to Lake Geneva, Wisconsin in October. We met with a group of elders associated with the Chicago church. They encouraged us to step down from leadership at Fellowship Bible Church and move to the Chicago area. They promised to support us financially as we made the expensive move. I had people encouraging me to stay at Fellowship Bible Church and fight. I had people encouraging me to start a new church in Fort Wayne. I knew after 14 years it was time to stop. On November 3, I announced my resignation from Fellowship Bible Church effective November 24. I'll never forget the seven year old boy with tears in his eyes when he heard the news. We left Fellowship Bible Church with all bills paid and a good amount in savings. I was blessed to turn over the church to a good man from Chicago. No one could take away many happy memories of God's faithfulness to us over the past 14 years. Our most trying year waited just ahead.

Overview of 14 years of Ministry at
Fellowship Bible Church

Romans 8:28 says these familiar words, *"And we know that God causes all things to work together for good to those who love God, to those who are called according to His purpose."* I am amazed, many years later, to look back and see God's faithfulness to the ministry of Fellowship Bible Church. God was faithful and He helped Fran and me to be faithful for 14 years. I asked a veteran pastor how long he had stayed in his church. He told me 14 years. I was just starting out and I couldn't believe any pastor could stay in one church for 14 years. I asked him why he stayed for 14 years. He simply said, "I stayed because it takes a while to see how people are going to turn out." Pastor Bob Yawberg told me that pastors leave churches too soon. I believe God created the church to be a family. The sheep can run off or be transferred to another pen but the true shepherd needs to remain faithful to whatever sheep God provides.

It is amazing to realize that the Apostle Paul probably stayed with the carnal Corinthian Church for several years. They were babies, took each other to court, got drunk at the communion table, practiced division and even questioned Paul's apostleship but Paul remained faithful to love them through God's faithful love and grace. I would not be the pastor I am today at Love Church if it wasn't for the 14 years I spent attempting to lead Fellowship Bible Church. I would ask forgiveness for anyone I hurt in leadership at Fellowship Bible Church. I thank God for everyone who helped make our ministry at Fellowship Bible Church possible. That ministry is still bearing fruit today.

Chapter 10 deals with God's faithfulness through the 21 plus years of ministry of Love Church of Fort Wayne. Though times have changed, the faithfulness of God has not changed. I remember a pastor told me about our ministry at Love Church. He said, "Mortensen, you're doing the job." I appreciated his kind words. The truth is God loves the poor and needy and He will provide for those who show them His love. Let's review God's faithfulness to

159

Love Church. Praise God that He uses all things for good for those who love Him and do His will.

CHAPTER 10

GOD'S FAITHFULNESS THROUGH LOVE CHURCH OF FORT WAYNE

SCRIPTURES RELATING TO CHAPTER 10

GOD'S FAITHFULNESS THROUGH
LOVE CHURCH OF FORT WAYNE

Luke 10:27, 28 – *"And he answered, 'You shall love the Lord your God with all your heart and with all your soul, and with all your strength, and with all your mind; and your neighbor as yourself.' And He said to him, 'you have answered correctly; Do this and you will live.'"*

John 11:36 – *"So the Jews were saying, "See how He loved Him!"*

John 21:17 – *"He said to him the third time, 'Simon, son of John, do you love Me?' Peter was grieved because he said to him the third time, 'Do you love me?' And he said to Him, 'Lord you know all things; You know that I love you.' Jesus said to him, 'Tend my sheep/'"*

Psalms 84:11 – *"For the Lord God is a sun and shield; The Lord gives grace and glory; No good thing does He withhold from those who walk uprightly."*

Philippians 1:6 – *"For I am confident of this very thing, that He who began a good work in you will perfect it until the day of Christ Jesus."*

I Corinthians 13:13 – *"But now faith, hope and love, abide these three; but the greatest of these is love."*

1Corinthians 16:14 – *"Let all that you do be done in love."*

Deuteronomy 6:4-7 – *"Hear, O Israel! The Lord is our God, the Lord is one! You shall love theLord you God with all your heart and with all your soul and with all your might."*

CHAPTER 10

GOD'S FAITHFULNESS THROUGH
LOVE CHURCH OF FORT WAYNE

God's Word tells us two major things about the nature of God. God is holy and God is love. We, as His church, need to demonstrate both His holiness and His love to others so they can come to know Him personally. God is faithful to provide to any ministry that reflects His nature of holiness and love. God's Word tells us in I Corinthians 13:13 that of faith hope and love, that love is the greatest. "Demonstrated love" demonstrates the very nature of God. Jesus gave three commandments to His church and they all revolve around demonstrating love to God, our neighbors and ourselves. Love that is not demonstrative and practical is not truly love at all.

Jesus Christ came to this earth to please His Heavenly Father by demonstrating God's love in many practical ways. People were hungry, so Jesus fed them. People were sick, so Jesus healed them. People needed to be forgiven of their sins, so Jesus forgave them. People needed salvation, so Jesus provided salvation through His death, burial and resurrection. The God of holiness and love is a very practical God. He can be reached by those who truly come to Him by faith; humbly expressing their needs.

Today God has raised up The Church, headed by His Son Jesus Christ, to truly demonstrate His love in the same practical ways. People need the Lord and the love He offers through His visible Church. This chapter deals with a local church family named Love Church, raised up by God to demonstrate His love to the poor and needy. It is also the story of a city-wide church working together to help make this effort a reality. The contents of this chapter will summarize the efforts of God's people in the greater Fort Wayne, Indiana area over these past 21 years. It is written to educate and motivate God's people to make a real difference in the lives of the poor and needy. God loves the poor and needy and He will provide in many practical ways for those who show them His love. Our mission field is not primarily the poor and needy, but the Church of Jesus Christ to help God's people show His love and be blessed as we demonstrate His love to the needy.

1986

Luke 22:42 – "Father, if You are willing, remove this cup from Me, yet not My will, but Yours be done."

Events to Remember and Quotes to Ponder

- My first written comment in my diary on January 1, 1986 said these words, "I'm doing God's will – hard, but good." I never realized the truth of these words that were about to come to pass in the following 365 days. I praise God for the Fort Wayne relationships that I made outside of Fellowship Bible Church. God has used many of these relationships and those outside of Fort Wayne to help make our ministry of showing God's love to the poor and needy possible. I would sincerely encourage pastors to make many friends inside and outside of their local church family.

- **"I QUIT" Pastor Phil said these two words many times.** We put our house up for sale in early January. Gary and Barb Warrick opened up their home for our son Michael to live while he attended the 11th grade at Willowbrook High School in the Chicago area. I would live with my parents in Wheaton, Illinois attempting to sell life and health insurance. Fran and Mary Ann would stay in Fort Wayne until the house was sold. Fran felt like a single mother with me coming home only on weekends. She and Mary Ann ate a lot of soup. Fran worked a low paying full-time job. We received $15.00 per month in food stamps. Our family finances were going from bad to worse. We had to cash a small retirement check to survive. We lived off of charge cards and the kindness of a few people who sent us finances. We met 18 leaders in Lake Geneva, Wisconsin who promised to send us finances. Only two of the 18 kept their promise. The final severance check from Fellowship Bible Church was almost $3,000.00 less than what we expected. After all, we had left the church with $30,000 in

165

the church savings account. I was in despair. I shared with Garry Warrick of my hurts. He said something I'll never forget. He said, "We're going to find out what kind of Christian Phil really is." It was exactly what I needed to hear.

- The house did not sell and I eventually returned to Fort Wayne. It was great to be home. Four months later we began Love Church. It began on September 7, 1986 in the living room of Ralph Moon. There were 44 people in attendance. We began our ministry as a united couple.

- My beloved father went to be with the Lord on October 17.

- We concluded 1986 knowing that God is my provider and I'm doing His will; even though I considered this year the most difficult year of my life.

1987

Luke 10:27 – "And he answered, You shall love the Lord your God with all your heart, and with all your soul, and with all your strength and with all your mind; and your neighbor as yourself."

Events to Remember and Quotes to Ponder

- We started 1987 in great shape. I was thrilled to be back in Fort Wayne with my wife and two children. Fran and I were both working full-time jobs and I was doing well at Huntington College working on my master's degree. Things at Love Church were going well. We averaged about 50 in the Sunday evening service and we enjoyed our rented facility at 505 E. Washington Street in downtown Fort Wayne. Fran and I enjoyed attending the morning service at Broadway Christian Church. They had a heart that reached out beyond racial and class lines.

- Our total church weekly rent was $100.00 including everything. The major drawback was the fact that the landlord had a "For Sale" sign on the building. We had one week to move if the landlord was able to find a buyer. We had to trust the Lord, and we did. Our agreed salary was $0.00 for the first 12 months. I did not want any demon to be able to accuse me about the motivation for starting Love Church.

- We took in approximately $12,000.00 the first six months of 1987. Fran expressed her frustration in having to work full-time, be a pastor's wife and try to take care of the house responsibilities all at the same time. I encouraged her to give two-weeks notice and quit work on August 14. On August 12, my fine Christian boss came to me and told me that due to slow business I would have to be let go. My date of termination was – you guessed it – August 14. Our church family said that they would support us financially

167

but finances were very limited. Barb Doughman said these words to me. "Phil, do what God has put in your heart to do." I knew I had to trust God for full-time financial support. I had to trust God for 100 days of full-time support. February 26, 2008 marked 7,500 days of full-time support.

- We began a Sunday morning service with the blessing of Broadway Christian Church and had 15 in attendance that first Sunday. 1987was a wonderful year to learn to trust God and to love people.

1988

Matthew 16:18 – "...I will build My church;..."

Events to Remember and Quotes to Ponder

- Two of our dear friends in ministry are John and Jane Sullivan from Christian Praise and Fellowship Church. They have been greatly used of God to reach out to thousands of men and women behind bars all over the world. Jane gave a great word from the Lord when she said, "God is laying a foundation at Love Church." Jesus was building His Church through the efforts of Love Church. We saw visitors coming on a regular basis. We had many people literally coming in off the streets to our downtown location.

- I remember a young man came to one of our Sunday night services on crutches. He stayed for about 15 minutes and then began to leave. I followed him out the door and asked him if he was feeling OK. He said something to me that I will never forget about our ministry. He said, "Mister there is so much love in that church, I can't stand it." Years later I understand what the gentleman was trying to say.

- Another man came into the facility demanding food for himself and his dog. We gave him a bag of groceries and he inspected each item. He left half of the items on the table and never even said "Thank you." The dog he brought in urinated on our one and only rug and the man didn't even express any sort of apology before he left. That stranger and that dog really helped me to know why we are helping the needy. We don't help the poor primarily because we love the poor or because we expect gratitude from them. We seek to help the poor because we love the Lord Jesus Christ and desire to follow His example.

- We saw attendance figures and church finances rise. We were blessed to be able to baptize a number of people into Christ.

- We were able to purchase a used wheel-chair van to help physically-challenged individuals attend church services.

- My personal highlight of the year was attending the Conflict Management course at Huntington College. The visiting instructor told me that it was OK to be "me" as leader of our church family. It was almost like getting saved again after the tremendous struggles I had with self-esteem for years at Fellowship Bible Church.

1989

Colossians 1:18 – "He is also head of the body, the church; and He is the beginning, the firstborn from the dead, so that He Himself will come to have first place in everything."

Events to Remember and Quotes to Ponder

- Nineteen eighty-nine started with the wedding of an inner-city couple that I had counseled for six weeks. The wedding went off without a hitch. The next morning the groom called me on his honeymoon. He said, "It's not going to work, preacher." He was right. The marriage dissolved in less than six months. Good marriages are hard to find anywhere but especially in the inner-city. There are few good role models to follow. This is one reason a couple with a stable marriage can be such a blessing to inner-city people. Fran and I have "intense fellowship" from time-to-time but our 42 plus years of marriage (as of 2007) give us unique credibility to speak into other marriages. You can't speak what you don't model.

- There were many blessing in 1989. Both of our children were involved in foreign mission trips.

- I graduated and earned a master's degree from Huntington College on May 13.

- We had visitor 1,000 attend our services.

- Doris Poling began attending. That started a journey of service to others for the past 19 years with us.

- Fran was able to work part-time for a Christian dentist. I was a part-time crossing guard to help with family finances. Nobody was getting rich but we were having a good time serving where God placed us.

- I was selected as the vice-president of the Fort Wayne Association of Evangelicals.

- We had the privilege of returning to Beaver Island, Michigan to minister to some hurting people in a non-denominational church.

- I felt that one of the highlights of the year was the development of a ministry called Kid's Club. This lasted four years under the leadership of Mike Spencer, youth pastor of Aboite Missionary Church. This fruitful effort brought both the inner-city children and suburban young people together in a joint venture which is still bearing fruit today. I would love to see more joint partnership efforts.

1990

Hebrews 13:20, 21a – "Now the God of peace, who brought up from the dead the great Shepherd of the sheep through the blood of the eternal covenant, even Jesus our Lord, equip you in every good thing to do His will..."

Events to Remember and Quotes to Ponder

- The church year verses for 1990 tell us that God has equipped His people to do His will. I have seen with my own eyes the faithfulness of God to provide everything for His people to fulfill His will in ministry. People will come and go but God is faithful to His Word. On January 22, I lost my beloved mother when God took her to heaven. She was a wonderful woman and a testimony of God's love to everyone she met. She never expressed bitterness at God for her lengthy battle with asthma. She showed God's love to the good people of Love Church whenever she was able to visit. She showed a great love to Fran which Fran appreciated in return. She was a great listener and a wonderful wife to my father for over 50 years. Life must go on, and it did following mom's funeral.

- We had several mentally-challenged individuals who became a real part of our church family. I was teaching one Sunday morning on the type of people found in the Bible that Jesus would help today if He met them in Fort Wayne. I listed robbers, tax collectors, lepers and women who lived as prostitutes. Louise (one of the special young ladies) raised her hand in church and asked me what a prostitute was. I tried to explain that a prostitute sold her body for sex. Louise responded with these words, "Pastor Phil, I would never be a prostitute. In fact if any guy tried to have sex with me, I would kick him where it hurts. Do you know what I mean?" I assured her that I did know what she meant. I loved her honesty and simple ways in the Lord.

- We started working together with other church families in ministry. This included passing out bread, having city-wide unity services, and blessing many needy people for Thanksgiving. We were finding out that it was OK to function as a local church and still be a part of what God was doing in the city-wide church at the same time.

1991

Genesis 12:3 – "And in all the families of the earth will be blessed."

Events to Remember and Quotes to Ponder

- Our verse for 1991 was a special blessing to me. I was raised to believe (from a very practical standpoint) that God only wanted to bless our local church family or people who dressed like us, talked like us, felt like us, believed exactly like us and sang out of the same hymn books as us every Sunday morning. **Think of it!** It truly was God's desire to bless every family on earth through Abram. Many churches apparently have a viewpoint that says, "We'll bless you if you bless us first." I have heard a number of Christians say to me, "Why should we help someone in need if they don't or won't attend our local church?" Romans 2:4 (KJV) says, *"the goodness of God leadeth thee to repentance."* God sends His rain on the just and the unjust according to Matthew 5:45. The Doxology reminds us that all blessings flow from God. Jesus desires to use His church to bless others in need.

- In 1991 God sent a woman into our church family who would have a great influence on all of us. Her name was Constance Williams. I could ask her how she was doing and no matter what her circumstances were, she would respond with just three words, "I am blessed!" She was blessed, no matter what. We were blessed to know her for seven wonderful years. God took her home to heaven in 1998 but I will never be the same. She was not a perfect woman but she concentrated on what she had (which truthfully wasn't much in material things) and not on what she didn't have.

- This is the year I broke my shoulder in two places while jogging in Foster Park. It was a painful lesson in learning to be more careful.

- We had a lady suffer a mental breakdown in church. She needed seven E.M.S. workers to help her get needed help. She is now doing great, knowing the unconditional love of Jesus for her.

- Our church family worked with God's people from 45 different church families.

- Constance Williams was right. She was blessed and so was all of Love Church. Zachariah 8:13 says that Israel was saved to be a blessing. That's how we see us.

- Our son Michael blessed us by graduating from Taylor University-Upland in 1991.

1992

Romans 8:28b – "Called according to His purpose"

Events to Remember and Quotes to Ponder

- I started the New Year with a major throat infection. The throat doctor didn't want me to preach or teach for six weeks. It's hard to argue with your wife when you cannot use your voice. Fran had to do double duty during my recovery period. She is a wonderful help-mate and God knows I need the help.

- I made an important Biblical discovery during my recovery time. I got a red-letter Bible and wrote down everything Jesus said. I grouped His words in individual categories. I discovered that in the books of Matthew, Mark and Luke Jesus talked more about the kingdom of God than any other subject. In the book of John He talked primarily about His relationship with His Heavenly Father. That study has really helped me to understand the ministry priorities of Jesus – God's kingdom and His relationship with God the Father.

- Fran literally helped save a baby girl's life in delivery. She has been used of God in so many ways. God has placed her in Love Church and she loves serving here.

- I received a word from the Lord that He placed the idea of Love Church in seed form in my heart in 1969 when I fully surrendered my life to do God's will.

- I had the privilege of helping marry my son Michael David to Christine LaRue on June 20 at the historic First Mennonite Church in Berne, Indiana. Robin LaRue, father of Christine, is also a pastor and we worked together throughout the beautiful ceremony. Christine has been such a blessing to Michael in their ministry over the years.

177

- We conducted our first walk-a-thon in Foster Park on Labor Day. We have been able through the years to raise funds for our vital transportation ministry through the walk-a-thon efforts. Its fun seeing people from various churches help us to help others in need.

- We were able to bless a growing number of people for Thanksgiving and Christmas.

- Our church family was growing steadily and more church families were choosing to help us.

1993

Revelation 3:18b – "...anoint your eyes so that you may see."

Events to Remember and Quotes to Ponder

- Every January a large group of pro-life marchers come together in Fort Wayne to march for the rights of unborn children. It is good to see several thousand people coming together from a wide variety of churches to support this effort. We have approximately 50,000 to 100,000 professing Christians in our community. Supporting pro-life causes is one of the many things we can do in unity, despite our differences. Many years ago one major denomination made a sincere effort to stop the spread of gambling in the state of Indiana. Sadly, the majority of Christians did not work together effectively. As a result, the lottery, river-boat gambling and horse track betting has taken millions of dollars away from the ability of the church to really help the poor and needy. It is such a tragedy to see people buying $40.00 worth of lottery tickets and not feed their family. Our society suffers when God's people refuse to work together and we allow minor differences to hinder our effectiveness to be salt and light, wherever God has placed us.

- I was privileged to speak at Concordia Lutheran Seminary to students working on their doctor's degree. The students seemed to have a real interest in knowing more about our ministry to the poor and needy.

- The major highlight of the year was the birth of our first grandchild, Andre David Philip Mortensen. He was healthy, big and beautiful.

- Love Church enjoyed some success with our church services being taped and shown on the local access television.

- God raised up a group of men to serve as new elders and deacons. I waited eight years to select these men and it was worth the wait.

- I heard H. B. London speak on the importance of accountability. We'll talk more about accountability in Chapter 13 but it was a real mile-stone in my personal life and in my ministry.

- A kind couple donated one of their inner-city homes to us for ministry.

- We concluded the year with Thanksgiving and Christmas blessings.

1994

Deuteronomy 28:2 – "All these blessing will come upon you and overtake you if you obey the Lord your God."

Events to Remember and Quotes to Ponder

- We began the New Year by making necessary repairs to our Love Mission House at 1905 E. Pontiac St. Our faithful servant, Doris Poling, moved into the house and became the director of the ministry to provide emergency housing for women in need. The challenge was that Doris was so busy at Love Church that she honestly didn't have the time to help run two ministries concurrently. We chose to have Doris concentrate on Love Church. Several women stayed briefly at the house over the years. Housing for the poor is a major need in Fort Wayne – especially for women. No one church family, no matter how large, can do everything. Each church family needs to seek God about it's priorities of ministry. I wish we could do more in the area of housing for the poor but God is rising up other ministries for this needy purpose. Barb Urbine, who was formerly homeless, was on of the greatest blessings to our ministry until the Lord took her home to heaven. She would often start her humble prayers with these words, "Dear Lord, this is Barb Urbine. I live at 141 East State in Fort Wayne." I know the Lord appreciated Barb reminding Him of her address. We miss her terribly. We would have missed a blessing if someone hadn't invited her to attend Love Church.

- Fran and I had the privilege of flying to the nation of Curacao with our dear friends, Ansel and Nani Aiken, for a week of ministry. We were shown much kindness by the people of Curacao.

- Fran and Doris Poling drove hundreds of miles to West Virginia looking for a runaway teen-ager.

- We were preparing to buy a box truck when a suburban church blessed us with theirs. That truck was a great blessing in helping with food, clothes and appliances.

- The year ended with many being helped with Thanksgiving and Christmas blessings.

- I love the variety of opportunities God has provided that allows us to show Christ's love to the poor and needy.

1995

Revelation 3:2a – "Wake up, and strengthen the things that remain.."

Events to Remember and Quotes to Ponder

- We began 1995 by thanking God for 100 months of blessing on our ministry to the poor and needy. It is such a thrill seeing people, once considered "dysfunctional", greatly used of God in humble service with Love Church.

- We were blessed with our first grand-daughter, Ashlyn Christine Mortensen, born on January 22.

- I was greatly ministered to personally at the Nappanee Conference in Nappanee, Indiana. The speaker talked about the pain of losing a church once considered very successful. He was driving a truck for a living at the time of his message. I sincerely thanked God for the pains we experienced at Fellowship Bible Church. His message brought a lot of healing and comfort to me as I literally cried out to God in my tears. We need to thank God for the hard times God uses in our lives.

- Fran shared with me that she finally felt that my priorities were changing - putting the family first and ministry second. I was blessed that she noticed the change and gave me that word of encouragement.

- I was given a very special 50th birthday surprise with many guests.

- Our daughter, Mary Ann, had her life spared after a potentially very serious car accident on U.S. Highway 30, west of Fort Wayne. She was bruised but we were blessed that she narrowly escaped serious injury. God was watching out for her.

- Fran and I had the opportunity to visit beautiful Island Royal National Park in far northern Michigan for our 30th anniversary.

- I was invited to attend a four-day prayer summit in Holland, Michigan. I couldn't believe you could get a group of pastors and leaders to pray for four days, but I really wanted to check it out. I'll talk more about it in Chapter 14 but let me say it was a great experience.

- I had a former youth pastor come to my door and offer sincere apology for his conduct several years previously. I was blessed by his honesty and his courage. I have had many opportunities to offer my apology to people that I have hurt over the years and it was not easy to do. I know God is pleased when His people make it right with each other.

- Someone placed a $15,000.00 check in the offering to help us finish in the black.

1996

Ephesians 3:20 – "Now to Him who is able to do far more abundantly beyond all that we ask or think, according to the power that works within us,"

Events to Remember and Points to Ponder

- In the early part of the year I was privileged to attend the Promise Keepers Pastor's Conference in Atlanta, Georgia. There were approximately 40,000 pastors in attendance, making it one of the largest gatherings of pastors in the history of the church. I praise God for using Promise Keepers to bring men together from many different church backgrounds. I attended my first service at the Jewish Temple upon my return to Fort Wayne.

- I got involved in a new organization called Pastors Uniting. This was an attempt to bring pastors together for discussion and eventual friendship development. Through this organization I met Tom and Linda Szymczak. They came from a strong Roman Catholic tradition. They have become some of our very closest friends in ministry. They have both taught our dear people and have received much love from them in return. I don't agree with everything their church believes but I know we have much more in common than I was raised to believe.

- On a personal note, I continued to enjoy jogging, but my marathon career was over. Fran and I spent some good time in Mio, Michigan. Mio is in the beautiful northern part of Michigan. Fran has many good memories of her childhood in the area due mainly to the kindness of her grandparents.

- I attended my second Pastor's Prayer Summit. There were several pastors who wept as they shared their hurting hearts with other pastors.

- We had our annual banquet at Taylor University – Fort Wayne with 450 in attendance. We celebrated ten wonderful years of ministry with many friends from a variety of church families. Ed Foley shared his testimony. Ed was a successful business man who attended a suburban church that was very supportive of us. He told us how teaching a class of inner-city boys at Love Church truly impacted his life.

Annual Banquet at Taylor University-Fort Wayne

- I heard Bill Wilson, who works with 20,000 inner-city kids in New York City, challenge us to make a difference. I wept as God encouraged me to remain faithful. We need each other if we are really going to make a difference in the inner-city. We need to work together if we're going to be obedient to Christ's prayer in John 17.

Galatians 5:13 – "For you were called to freedom brethren; only do not turn your freedom into an opportunity for the flesh, but through love serve one another."

Events to Remember and Quotes to Ponder

- A dear friend of mine, Arlen Friesen, once said, "Love Church is a miracle from God." Nineteen ninety-seven would truly be a miracle year for us and our ministry.

- Fran and I started the year off with a three-day retreat to Northern Ontario. We rode what they call the "Snow Train" through 100 miles of beautiful, snow-covered wilderness.

- Upon our return, we were told that we would need to look for another church facility because our rented facility was about to be sold. The landlord was very kind to us; never raising our weekly rent of $100.00 in nearly 12 years. We were already packed in our 4,400 square foot facility and it was getting time to move. An inner-city mother of six encouraged me to start a building fund. She told me that she would give the first dollar. I told her I would give $2.00 then I asked her, jokingly, "What kind of facility can we buy with $3.00?" We challenged our humble people to trust God as never before in financial giving. We passed out two giving envelopes each week. One envelope was for the general expenses of the church and the second one was for the church building fund. We collected $79.45 for the building fund in the last week of February of 1997. I talked to Steve Bostrom, one of our fine missionaries, about our need to raise at least $60,000.00 for a down payment on a future building. He gave me a great word. He said, "Don't seek $60,000.00. Seek the Lord and He will give you $60,000.00." The Lord put on my heart a huge warehouse of 43,000 square feet located at 1331 E.

Berry Street, in the inner-city, about a mile east of our downtown location. It was vacant and in need of much remodeling. I saw it as a great place that could serve as both a church facility and a facility for the Love Community Center which would offer GED training, computer and literacy classes as well as job training, exercise and woodshop ministry in the future. We hosted an open house and I challenged 30 pastors to help us raise the needed funds. On November 6, 1997 we wrote out a check for $359,000.00. The miracle was ours.

1331 East Berry Street –Fort Wayne, Indiana

1998

*I Chronicles 29:1 – "Then King David said to the entire
assembly, 'My son Solomon, whom alone God has chosen, is
still young and inexperienced and the work is great; for the
temple is not for man, but for the Lord God.'"*

Events to Remember and Quotes to Ponder

- We began the New Year with a new sense of excitement as
  to what God had in store for us. We cleaned out our
  warehouse facility at 1331 E. Berry but we couldn't have
  services there for many months and much remodeling. Our
  landlord at 505 E Washington, downtown, was kind to us
  and allowed us the opportunity to stay there until our new
  facility was ready.

- Many years ago I felt the Lord had said that our ministry
  would be a training center and in 1997 He helped us do it.
  We offer a 13-week urban ministry course which allows
  people to have a much better understanding of the inner
  city. Randy Dodge from Taylor University -Fort Wayne
  and his family are the first ones to take the course and pass
  it. They did a good job of getting to know our people
  better, and received a better understanding of what showing
  Christ's love in the inner-city is all about.

- We needed to raise approximately $150,000.00 to help us
  remodel the first floor which would allow us to have church
  services and Sunday school. One family blessed us with
  $50,000.00 to see this project completed. Christians from
  over 90 church families got involved in helping us. The
  key church to help us was New Hope United Methodist
  Church in Mecosta, Michigan. Mecosta is located 35 miles
  west of Mount Pleasant. We had approximately 30 people
  come and help us for two weeks. They did everything that
  we asked them to do, and more. When they were finished
  we had the kitchen, food shelf room, bathrooms, our

189

feeding room and classrooms completed. They also gave us $5,000.00 plus their hundreds of hours of free labor. That amazing week of service has led to a ten-year relationship of love between our two church families which continues today.

- On August 16, Christians from 33 church families marched together from our old location to our new location for our first Sunday morning worship service.

- Our landlord on East Washington gave us $10,000.00 to help us with remodeling expenses.

- We officially dedicated the building on September 27. Many churches were represented at the dedication.

- Thanksgiving was a special holiday this year as we reflected on God's goodness to us.

1999

John 17:3 – "This is eternal life, that they may know You, the only true God, and Jesus Christ whom You have sent."

Events to Remember and Quotes to Ponder

- The first Sunday of this year we had to cancel services because of excessive snow. Harlan Cabinets put in all new kitchen cabinets for us a few days later and they looked beautiful.

- We started to put together the organizational pieces for the future development of Love Community Center.

- We are constantly reaching out to pastors in an effort to build relationships.

- Jerry and Annie Gillum found an 88 year old woman while they were passing out bread in the inner-city neighborhood near our church facility. She began attending Love Church. She was later struck in the arm by a bullet from someone who mistakenly thought she had drugs in her humble home. She spent the last few years of her life in a nursing home. Our faithful drivers picked her up from the nursing home until she was 95 years old and very frail. The Lord took her to heaven. We miss Ruth Vining, and I thank God for the love the Gillums showed to her. God's love brought her to Love Church. There are many lonely people like her that need a church family.

- Our Christian Congressman, Mark Souder, remarked during his visit to our facility, "Pastor Phil, I don't know anyone in Fort Wayne putting you or your ministry down." I felt God blessed us with a good reputation in the community and that is important.

191

- Fran was honored by Taylor University—Fort Wayne with an honorary degree for 25 plus years of faithful urban service. She deserved it I was and still am very proud of her.

- We raised over $10,000.00 at our annual banquet to help with expenses.

- Josh and Justin, two Taylor University-Fort Wayne students, did a good job for us serving as summer interns. Huntington College students have also been a great blessing to us over the years. We deeply desire college students to be involved in our ministry.

- We had a very special baptism service with three churches involved. What made that so very special is that it was held at a very conservative church where African-Americans were not allowed to be baptized several years previously. It was a blessing seeing people from different racial and cultural backgrounds obeying the Lord in baptism.

2000

John 17:21 – "that they may all be one; even sa You, Father, are in Me and I in You, that they also may be in Us; so that the world may believe that You sent Me.:

Events to Remember and Quotes to Ponder

- We began our New Year with an excellent pastor's retreat at Pokagon State Park in Indiana.

- Mike Votaw and John Miller were a great help to us in remodeling the second floor for the future development of the Love Community Center.

- Father John Pfeister from Queen of Angels Catholic Church was one of our February Sunday night speakers. Father John became a good friend; choosing to be involved in the pastors' prayer summit. He shared his faith of knowing Jesus personally and his desire to help others come to know Him.

- I was especially moved to hear Pastor Bart Pierce from Baltimore, Maryland share of his visions for inner-city ministry. Tears do not come easy for me but I wept after hearing his heart and his challenge for inner-city united ministry to the poor and needy.

- Fran and I returned to Pontiac, Michigan to attend the memorial service at Marimont Church for a man who we both knew as teenagers in that church. I shared our urban missions experience in Fort Wayne over the past 30 years with several of the people whom I had known for many years. I felt they could not have cared less about us or our ministry. God spoke to my spirit with these words, "Do not grieve when others do not understand My calling on your life. I had to remove you from Pontiac for you to do My will in Fort Wayne." Those words have really been a comfort to me over the years. All ministry must be first to God and His will and then to people and their needs. I believe this is one of the keys to not becoming discouraged while working in the inner-city mission field. Jesus came to please His Heavenly Father in His ministry. He calls me and all of His servants to please Him first and He will take care of the rest.

- God gave me the privilege of teaching Taylor University-Fort Wayne students an introductory class on urban ministry. I felt it was a good experience and gave me a greater desire to impact young people with a heart for urban mission service.

2001

John 17:26 – "and I have made Your name known to them, and will make it known, so that the love with which You loved Me may be in them, and I in them."

Events to Remember and Quotes to Ponder

- God is so good in providing all of our needs, despite my fears and unbelief. In February Steve Gift began full-time ministry with us as our assistant pastor. Steve has many years of service in different areas of transportation including truck, bus and handicapped vehicles. Steve agrees to head up the transportation ministry of Love Church. We don't have city bus service in Fort Wayne on Sundays or much past 8:00 p.m. Many of our people cannot afford their own vehicle so we need to provide transportation for them to attend our church services.

- Ralph Moon continued to be a blessing; heading up the maintenance ministry of our church.

- Doris Poling continues to serve faithfully in the areas of music, food and clothing.

- Fran headed up the considerable administrative efforts.

- I praise God for the full-time team of workers with a common vision of serving the Lord as we demonstrate together His love to the poor and needy.

- Twelve of our people were privileged to drive to Tampa, Florida to visit the amazing inner-city ministry of Without Walls International Church. I have more to say about this good ministry in Chapter 15. Let me just say that the visit had a great influence on those who were able to make the trip. Let me encourage the reader to visit inner-city church ministries for yourself. Jesus was *"...moved with compassion.."* when He saw the needy multitudes. (KJV – Matthew 9:36) We need to see for ourselves the needy individuals right where they live, so that God can move our hearts for service.

- I watched in horror to see the Twin Towers in NYC come down on September 11, resulting in the deaths of almost 3,000 people. The real tragedy is that multiplied thousands of people are murdered every year in the inner-cities of America and hardly a cry can be heard. A Chicago television station recently reported that more children were murdered on their way to school in Chicago than Chicago soldiers killed in Iraq.

2002

Nehemiah 2:20 – "The God of heaven will give us success."

Events to Remember and Quotes to Ponder

- We began the New Year with the offering of exercise classes upstairs. Exercise equipment was donated through our good friend Dale Hanson from Blackhawk Ministries.

- My annual physical went well in February despite my long battle with migraine headaches.

- A Christian television reporter offers to make a video of our ministry for promotion.

- Fran and I take a course offered by the Fort Wayne Police Department. We spent eleven Monday nights together learning more about what police personnel actually go through on a daily basis in dealing with the public. I would recommend every pastor to better know your police personnel in your community.

- I made a wooden bowl in the Community Center woodshop. It took me six and one-half hours to complete, even with Ralph Moon's help. It made me feel good that I could make something with my own hands. We need people experienced in woodworking to help inner-city people make something with their hands.

- We had almost 1,000 people attend our neighborhood outreach carnival. It was great seeing many parts of God's church working together demonstrating God's love to others in need.

- A local foundation gave the Community Center a grant for $31,000.00 to help us with our computer ministry. I would challenge every church family to prayerfully consider

197

offering some type of computer assistance to those in need. We have seen at least nine individuals get full-time jobs as a result of the training we offered to them.

- We had a good four-day tent meeting bringing several church families together for outreach to our needy neighbors. We probably had more mosquitoes in attendance than people but I would do it again if the Lord leads us to do so.

- Other highlights for 2002 included a gathering of 79 pastors and leaders for our four-day prayer summit in Holland, Michigan.

- George Krestik gave a wonderful message for our anniversary Sunday.

- Beacon Light Chapel sponsored a pig roast for us. Everyone had a great time but the pig.

- A Christian businessman donated a nice van to Fran. We ended the year with a great unity service.

2003

II Corinthians 13:5 – "Test yourselves to see if you are in the faith; examine yourselves! Or do you not recognize this about yourselves, that Jesus Christ is in you—unless indeed you fail the test?"

Events to Remember and Points to Ponder

- A wonderful city-wide praise rally started off the New Year. Many church families participated in worshiping together.

- I had the opportunity to teach on urban ministry to my second class of students from Taylor University—Fort Wayne.

- Fran and I flew to Phoenix, Arizona for a Promise Keepers Pastors' Conference. I was blessed to see charismatic and non-charismatic pastors working together in harmony honoring one another.

- I later spent considerable time encouraging another Fort Wayne inner-city pastor who was converting a bar into a church ministry reaching out to another needy urban neighborhood. He is being blessed of God today for his desire for accountability and co-operation across racial and denominational lines.

- I am blessed with a couple, Dave and Jennifer Stemen, who are serving the needy through Love Church. They come from a suburban evangelical background actually living out in the country 25 miles from our church facility. They have faithfully taught our inner-city young people for many years. They felt God wanted them to adopt special needs children from different racial backgrounds. What a blessing and what a difference this couple has made in the young lives of children who would be considered as "rejects" in our comfortable society. These children have been a great blessing despite their challenges to the Stemen family and to Love Church. I would encourage pastors to prayerfully consider challenging their people to seek God about bringing such a child into their home as their own.

- Fran and I were blessed to see our daughter Mary Ann graduate from Indiana University—Fort Wayne. She worked hard to get her degree and we are proud of her heart to help needy individuals.

- We conducted a funeral for a 35-year old mother who had previously given birth to a baby girl as a result of a rape.

- I had the privilege of going to Philadelphia with a group of Fort Wayne Pastors to see what they are doing to promote city-wide prayer efforts and co-operation. It was a very encouraging experience.

2004

Romans 8:28 – "And we know that God causes all things to work together for good to those who love God, to those who are called according to His purpose."

Events to Remember and Points to Ponder

- Fran and I began the New Year serving as speakers for a youth retreat in Wisconsin Dells, Wisconsin. Upon our return home, I received a phone call from an ex-offender in Parkview Hospital. I visited him and asked him why he was in the hospital. He told me he tried to commit suicide after not being able to find a job due to his prison record. I would encourage employers to give ex-offenders an opportunity to prove themselves when they have a job opening by hiring them. They should not automatically be disqualified because of their past. Almost eighty per-cent of ex-offenders return to prison after their release. Failure to find employment is one of the major reasons for this return.

- Shane Meredith is hired part-time at Love Church serving as our worship leader.

- Deacon Dennis and Mardeen escaped a serious midnight fire that destroyed their apartment. God restored their belongings through the kindness of concerned neighbors and Love Church.

- A single mother with four children, previously living in our building when she was homeless, was selected top graduate out of 177 individuals from a local college.

- Deb Kennedy serves Fran with her computer skills.

- New Hope Methodist Church comes and helps paint our facility.

- A good number of volunteers from various churches helped us bag 1,120 bags of groceries for distribution.

- We visited a sweet girl by the name of Chrissy. She is blind with many physical challenges but she has a great sense of humor and blesses everyone who comes to visit her.

- A local trucking firm headed by a wonderful Christian made trucks available for our use.

- Pastor couples meet on the first Monday of each month for a Dutch-treat meal at a local restaurant. We are blessed to have many friends.

2005

Ephesians 4:15 – "but speaking the truth in love, we are to grow up in all aspects into Him who is the head, even Christ."

Events to Remember and Quotes to Ponder

- Fran began the New Year with successful colon cancer surgery. A group of pastors offer to help with expenses not covered by insurance. We're blessed with many friends bringing in meals for us.

- Many church families get involved with a city-wide effort called "Reach for More." This effort allowed Christians to minister to over 10,000 kids in the public school system. Speakers spoke about pre-marital sex, drugs and the need for strong moral values. Students were invited to attend a youth rally at the Fort Wayne Coliseum on a Sunday night to hear more about the person of Jesus Christ who could help them to change their life. Thousands of young people attended the youth rally and many gave their life to Christ. It showed the power of a united church effort. I would strongly encourage churches to work together in similar efforts to impact the public schools. It's not enough to complain about how bad things are in the public schools. Many of the school systems are willing to work with God's people.

- We had 54 church families represented at our annual banquet.

- Karl Kaletta, a blind man from Love Church, was greatly used of God as he showed DVD's in a local nursing home. Karl is now with Jesus but he did make a real difference in the lives of many individuals, in spite of his handicaps.

- I was blessed to perform the wedding of our daughter Mary Ann to Andre' Goodwell in July at Broadway Christian Church. The wedding was beautiful.

- Gospel singer Larry Ford was a great blessing as he ministered to Love Church in song. He told me we ought to change the name of our church to "Warehouse of Love" – Not a bad suggestion.

- A local church donates over 3,000 pounds of food for our food shelf ministry.

- Rich Coulter, our new maintenance man, and I were privileged to visit over 50 churches in 2005.

- Love Church continues to be a blessing with Thanksgiving and Christmas goodies.

2006

Romans 1:7a – "to all who are beloved of God in Rome, called as saints;"

Events to Remember and Quotes to Ponder

- I began the New Year ministering in a new church effort in Harrison, Michigan. The pastor is Jim Noggle, who was such a blessing to us when he pastored at New Hope United Methodist in Mecosta, Michigan.

- Our freezer/cooler is a great blessing to our ministry in assisting the poor and needy with their food needs. This was donated by our friends in Holland, Michigan, where our annual prayer summits are held.

- Fran and I prepared to go to Israel with our dear friends from Woodburn Missionary Church. We had never been to Israel but it turned out to be a great experience for both of us. God's Word really came alive as we were able to visit various Biblical sites in both Israel and Jordan. Fran was re-baptized in the Sea of Galilee by Pastor Joel DeSelm of Woodburn Missionary Church. I was able to sit on the very steps at the temple in Jerusalem where Jesus ministered. I would strongly encourage every pastor to seek God about the possibility of visiting the Holy Land. It would be a great investment in your pastor and in your church. I can't explain how grateful I am for the opportunity Fran and I had to visit in the Holy Land. There is no place like it on the entire earth.

- Upon our return the city-wide church had a very special prayer time at eleven different sites across our community. We prayed a blessing over the land which has seen much blood-shed and injustice. We all met together for a powerful time of praise and worship that evening.

- A local Christian businessman blesses the Love Mission house with many brand new windows.

- Brian Grimes surprises me with a hot pizza during my Father's Day Sermon. This has become a tradition over the year and is greatly appreciated.

- A young man who spent 22 years in prison shares his testimony with me.

- Thirty volunteers passed out 125 sacks of bread to our needy neighbors who live in government housing.

- We received the final mailed donation of $25,000.00 which allowed us to finish 2006 in the black financially.

Galatians 6:10 – "So then, while we have opportunity, let us do good to all people, and especially of those who are of the household of the faith."

Events to Remember and Quotes to Ponder

- I was grateful to start the New Year with Fran at my side during her constant fight with cancer.

- Rich Coulter and I had the privilege of visiting over 150 church families in the area. These visits have allowed us to build new friendships for future ministry together. Virtually every church leader sincerely appreciated our visit. I would encourage pastors to spend some time each week and make a phone call, write a note, or visit another pastor in person in an effort to build a Christ-honoring relationship. It will be a great blessing to you.

- I spent three and one-half hours at lunch with a leader who had spent over 35 years in church planting in the suburban and rural communities of our nation. He recently received a burden from the Lord to help plant inner-city churches. We had a great lunch together.

- At the end of our accountability meeting, on January 31 at 8:30 AM, I told my pastor and accountability brother that I loved him. We had been meeting together for the past 14 years. He told me that he loved me and wished me a good day. He was called into the presence of Jesus on February 1. This was a sudden passing due to heart failure. There were 40 pastors, including me, at his funeral. I'm so glad God put Jim McCarty and me together. We honestly never had a cross word between us.

- I fasted 21 days and again 40 days for the glory of God to be revealed in my wife's body. I had two colonoscopies during the year showing no cancer. I would encourage my pastor friends to get an annual physical plus a colonoscopy when needed.

- We were able to trade our car with 234,000 miles with one with only 112,000 mile on it.

- We celebrated God's goodness on our 21st church anniversary on September 7.

- We ended the year blessing many needy folks with Thanksgiving and Christmas blessings.

2008

Matthew 6:33 – "But seek first His kingdom and His righteousness; and all these things will be added to you."

Goals for the Future

- Maintain my spiritual and physical life including weight control, daily devotions and seeking God and His presence in my daily life.

- Distribute this book to others who want to learn more about how to show Christ's love to the poor and needy through His Church.

- Make progress in helping to birth a future inner-city church, possibly on the South side of Fort Wayne, Indiana.

- I hope to continue to preach in one church per month outside of Love Church.

- Continue to raise needed funds for Love Church, Love Community Center, church roof repairs and for future ministry rooms. These rooms will provide temporary living quarters for Christian college students who desire to learn more about the inner-city by living in it.

I Corinthians 16:14 says, *"Let all that you do be done in love."* Our Love Church ministry has made a sincere effort to put that verse into practice over these past 21 plus years. God has been faithful to help us fulfill the purpose for which He designed us. Let's move on to Section IV and Chapter 11 entitled "Fifteen Lies Christians Often Believe That Hinder Inner-City Ministry." Satan is a liar and he has done and will do everything he can to try to stop Christ's Church from making a difference in the inner-city. Get ready for a very hard-hitting chapter. We overcome Satan's lies by putting God's truth into practice.

Let's Go!

SECTION IV

GOD'S TRUTH TO OVERCOME LIES THAT HINDER INNER-CITY MINISTRY

CHAPTER 11

FIFTEEN LIES THAT CHRISTIANS OFTEN BELIEVE THAT HINDER INNER-CITY MINISTRY

FIFTEEN LIES THAT CHRISTIANS OFTEN BELIEVE THAT HINDER INNER-CITY MINISTRY

<u>*Genesis 3:1*</u> – *"Now the serpent was more crafty than any beast of the field which the Lord God had made. And he said to the woman, "Indeed, has God said, 'You shall not eat from any tree of the garden?'"*

<u>*Psalms 119:160*</u> – *"The sum of Your word is truth, And every one of Your righteous ordinances is everlasting."*

<u>*John 1:14*</u> – *"And the Word became flesh, and dwelt among us, and we saw His glory as the only begotten from the Father, full of grace and truth."*

<u>*John 8:32*</u> – *"and you will know the truth, and the truth will make you free."*

<u>*John 8:44*</u> – *"You are of your father the devil, and you want to do the desires of your father. He was a murderer from the beginning, and does not stand in the truth, because there is no truth in him. Whenever he speaks a lie, he speaks from his own nature, for he is a liar, and the father of lies."*

<u>*John 16:13*</u> – *"But when He, the Spirit of truth, comes, He will guide you into all the truth; for He will not speak on His own initiative, but whatever He hears, He will speak; and He will disclose to you what is to come."*

<u>*John 17:17*</u> – *"Sanctify them in the truth; Your word is truth."*

<u>*Ephesians 4:15*</u> – *"but speaking the truth in love, we are to grow up in all aspects into Him, who is the head, even Christ."*

CHAPTER 11

FIFTEEN LIES THAT CHRISTIANS OFTEN BELIEVE THAT HINDER INNER-CITY MINISTRY

For many years I have asked various denominational leaders why their church organization has not been more aggressive in starting new inner-city churches or partnering with existing inner-city churches. One leader was honest and said that it was just too much effort to reach across cultural and racial barriers to plant inner-city churches. Most of the leaders had no answer for me. I met one young man who probably gave me the best answer. He said he believed it was simply demonic that more new churches are not being established in the inner-city.

God's Word warns believers over and over about the danger of being deceived. Matthew 24:4 (KJV) says, *"And He said, 'See to it that you are not misled;...'"* Paul writes to Christians in I Corinthians 3:18 with these words: *"Let no man deceive himself..."* John warns in II John 2:7 – *"For many deceivers have gone out into the world...."* James tells us in James 1:22, *"But prove yourselves doers of the Word, and not merely hearers who delude (KJV – deceive) themselves."* One of my major motivations to write this book is to inform professing Christians of God's love for the poor and needy. This love needs to be expressed in the formation of new churches in the rural, suburban and inner-city communities of our world. I love the Church of Jesus Christ that He is building around the world. I'm not an outsider taking pot-shots at God's people. I love God's church enough to be grieved by the fact that few inner-city churches are being started in proportion of the many new churches reaching out to the middle and upper-class communities of our nation.

I believe that the American evangelical church is simply being deceived by not doing what Jesus did or not obeying His commands by showing His love to the poor and needy. Please take the following true and false test that lists 15 statements many

Christians have practiced as truths in their lives. We are only set free by the truth of God by practicing it, not just saying we believe it.

Fifteen Lies vs. What God's Word Says About the Poor and Needy.

Note: Please circle or underline, in your opinion, the best answer.

1. True? or False?   "Showing God's love to the poor and needy is not my responsibility because I am not gifted by the Holy Spirit to do so." (I Corinthians 12:4-10, 28; Romans 12:6-8; Ephesians 4:8-11; I Corinthians 7:7; I Peter 4:9-11)

2. True? or False?   "It is not the responsibility of our Christian denomination to plant inner-city churches reaching out to the poor." (Luke 4:18)

3. True? or False?   "Planting churches exclusively for the middle-class and upper-class makes good business sense because the poor have no means to support the church financially and besides it's too dangerous to worship in the inner-city." (James 2:1-9)

4. True? or False?   "Helping the poor and needy means taking care of them regardless of their response." (II Thessalonians 3:10)

5. True? or False?   "Early Christians sold their possessions and land and gave their funds exclusively for the building fund." (Acts 2:45, 4:34-37)

6. True? or False?   "There is no relationship between the assurance of one's personal salvation and the act of providing for the physical needs of others." (I John 3:14-17)

7. True? or False?   "Jesus said He was well aware of the doctrinal statement of the church." (Revelation 2:2; 2:19; 3:1; 3:8; and 3:15)

8. True? or False?   "God is much too holy to be affected by how His people treat the poor and needy." (Proverbs 14:31)

9. True? or False?   "God is not obligated to financially reimburse those supportive of the poor." (Proverbs 19:17)

10. True? or False?   "God would never curse anyone simply for shutting his eyes to the needs of the poor." (Proverbs 28:27)

11. True? or False?   "Sodom was judged by God primarily for their sin of immorality." (Ezekiel 16:49)

12. True? or False?   "God guarantees His people in the Old Testament will never be judged by Him simply for not treating the poor and needy properly." (Amos 4:1-2)

13. True? or False?   "Jesus would never expect His followers to help the poor and needy just because He did it." (Matthew 28:18-20)

14. True? or False?   "Jesus said preaching the gospel to the poor was not an evidence of Him being the Messiah." (Luke 7:22)

15. True? or False?   "Jesus said those who called Him Lord would not be held accountable for not helping the poor and needy; especially if they failed to recognize Jesus through the needs of the poor as long as they said helping the poor wasn't their calling." (Matthew 25:41-47)

Let's find the correct answers by looking closer into God's Word

Question 1

"Showing God's love to the poor and needy is not my responsibility because I am not gifted by the Holy Spirit to do so."

–**FALSE**. I have listed the various places in the Bible where the diverse gifts and offices of the Holy Spirit are found. The reason the answer is false is because Biblically there is no such gift as helping the poor and needy. My primary gift is mercy and Fran's primary gift is administration. Fran and I don't help the poor and needy because we are gifted, Biblically, to do so. We don't come from an inner-city background. Our home church didn't teach us to help the poor and needy. In fact, people from other racial groups were not sought out by our church family as children. According to John 8:28-29, Jesus did everything He did to please His Heavenly Father. We help the poor and needy for the same reason – we want to please our Heavenly Father. Please don't hide behind the lie or the excuse that God doesn't expect you, as a Christian, to help the poor and needy just because you don't feel gifted to do so.

Question 2

"It is not the responsibility of our Christian denomination to plant inner-city churches reaching out to the poor."

218

–**FALSE**. The word "Christian" literally means "little Christ." As Christians we are to demonstrate the nature of Christ in our words and in our deeds. The first recorded words of Jesus, following His temptation in the wilderness, are recorded in Luke 4:18. Jesus said the Holy Spirit anointed Him to preach the gospel to the poor. The first priority of the ministry of Jesus was to preach God's Word to the poor. This passage is stated hundreds of years before and recorded in Isaiah 61:1-2. Jesus did preach the gospel to the poor. The Pharisees did not preach to the poor because they were motivated by money. (Luke 16:14) If Jesus fulfilled His responsibility to preach the gospel to the poor and to meet their physical needs, is it not fair to say that every Christian denomination has this same responsibility? Many Christian denominations began by reaching out to the poor. I know from personal experience of one denominational church that began by helping the poor and has remained faithful to that calling. That church denomination would be the Salvation Army; who minister to the poor and needy around the world. I have never been a part of their organization but I highly respect them.

Question 3

"Planting churches exclusively for the middle-class and upper-class makes good business sense because the poor have no means to support the church financially and besides it's too dangerous to worship in the inner-city."

–**FALSE**. The answer would be true if the Lord designed His Church to be a business. Praise God he designed it to be a family. God desires everyone to be a part of His family, regardless of income or class or racial background. James tells us in harsh terms that treating someone differently in church because of their riches indicates that the church is being motivated by evil motives. (James 2:1-9) James further tells us that God chose the poor of this world to be *"rich in faith and heirs of the kingdom..."* James further says in verse nine that showing favoritism to the rich is a sin against God. Neither the rich nor the poor are the source of church finances. God is our source and He will bless those who bless the poor and needy. The possibility of physical danger in the inner-city is not an excuse for failure to minister in obedience of God's call to the inner-city. Much of the American church is living as if the answer was true to this question. My God help His Church to change its ways.

Question 4

"Helping the poor and needy means taking care of them regardless of their response."

–**FALSE.** II Thessalonians 3:10 says, *"...if anyone is not willing to work, then he is not to eat, either."* Showing Christ's love to the poor and needy does not mean taking complete care of them, regardless of their response. A concerned family should not encourage laziness or irresponsibility. Let me give you an example of what I am trying to say. Fran received a phone call from an unknown woman asking for rental assistance. She gave a hard-luck story how she lost her job and didn't have the finances to take care of her children. She said that our church could write out the check to her landlord instead of her personally. The more Fran questioned her, the more lies came forth. Fran told her we would not help her with her request. Several months later this same woman was written up in the newspaper. She was going to prison for four years on fraud charges. Investigators found she was a former preacher's daughter and she scammed 60 churches out of benevolent funds. Her "landlord" was her live-in boyfriend. Many of those churches could have been spared a lot of grief by simply calling Fran and checking out the woman's story with her. Churches need to work together to stop cheaters from ripping off the church. Many churches hurt lazy people by giving in to their demands without getting to know them first. There are many poor people requesting help from churches with real needs. There are also many just trying to take advantage of the church. Like a good parent, a good church family needs to get to know a needy person before saying yea or no to their request.

Question 5

"Early Christians sold their possessions and land and gave their funds exclusively for the building fund."

–FALSE. In Acts 2:45 and Acts 4:34-37, God's people were moved by the Holy Spirit to sell some of their property and give the proceeds to the church leadership in order that every financial need of the people would be met. The American Church has spent over 500 billion dollars in the last ten years on church buildings with the poor having little benefit from these expenditures. Nice church buildings have their place. We must not forget that the church is primarily people that God loves and wants to use for His kingdom.

Question 6

"There is no relationship between the assurance of one's personal salvation and the act of providing for the physical needs of others."

–FALSE. The assurance of one's personal salvation is very important to the Christian believer. Evangelical Christians believe we are "saved" by confession of sin and trust in the death, burial and resurrection of Jesus Christ according to Romans 10:9, 10 and other references. The question needs to be asked, "How does a person have the assurance of their salvation?" Jesus said in Matthew 7:16 and 7:20 that they would be known by their fruit. Jesus further said in John 13:34, 35 that the assurance of one's salvation would be demonstrated by love for one another. James said in James 2:17, *"Even so faith, if it has no works, is dead, being by itself."* John said the assurance of our salvation is demonstrated by our love for one another. He further describes in I John 3:17 this love in practical terms; questioning a person's salvation if they are not willing to share their goods with others in need. The rich young ruler in Matthew 19:16-22 did not obtain eternal life because he was unwilling to sell his possessions, give the funds to the poor and follow Jesus. I cannot earn my salvation by helping the poor but I can demonstrate my salvation by helping the poor. Romans 5:5 tells us that God's love has been placed within our hearts. God's love within me, expressed to the poor, is major evidence that I have received God's free gift of salvation. I'm sure of it.

Question 7

"Jesus said He was well aware of the doctrinal statement of the church."

–**FALSE.** Having a Biblical foundation is essential for any church family that desires to please God. Having a statement of faith based on Biblical essentials is good. Jesus said to five different church families the same thing, *"I know your deeds."* In fact in Revelation 2:5 the church of Ephesus, who couldn't tolerate evil men, was rebuked by Jesus with these words: *"...repent and do the deeds you did at first;..."* Jesus further said in Matthew 5:16 that our good deeds would bring glory to the Father. It is not enough for a church to claim doctrinal purity. Hurting and needy people need to see a church living their Biblical doctrine in practical, loving ways.

Question 8

"God is much too holy to be affected by how His people treat the poor and needy."

–**FALSE.** The Bible says many times that *"God is holy."* The reason the answer is false is because God is affected by how the poor and needy are treated. Proverbs 14:31 says, *"He who oppresses the poor taunts his Maker, But he who is gracious to the needy honors Him."* There is a special bond between God and His creation, especially the poor. Those who oppress the poor are sinning against their creator. The work "taunts", used in this verse, means to mock, jeer or provoke. The word describes what Jesus endured on the cross when the people were taunting Him. **Think of it!** When the poor are mistreated by others, God is being mocked as their creator. The opposite is also true in this verse when it says that a person who is gracious to the needy honors God. God was so grieved by the violence on the earth that He sent a flood to destroy mankind. (Genesis 6:13) John 3:16 tells us that God was so affected by the needs of mankind that He sent His only begotten Son, Jesus, to into the world to save it. We don't work with the poor and needy as a church family primarily because we love the poor. We work with the poor and needy as a church family because we love the Lord and desire bring honor to Him by doing so. Thank God that He is affected by what is happening to the poor, good or bad. His Church needs also to be affected by how the poor and needy are being treated. Thank God for a Holy God who is concerned about people in need.

Question 9

"God is not obligated to financially reimburse those supportive of the poor."

FALSE. God's Word tells us in Proverbs 29:17 that God has obligated Himself to repay those who are gracious to the poor. In fact He says that love shown to the poor is love show to Him. **Think of it!** Proverbs 28:27a says those who give to the poor will never want (KJV:lack). It grieves me when an evangelical church says, "We cannot afford to help the poor and needy." Any church believing that lie will never receive the financial provision God has for them. I know God blesses those who bless the poor. We'll be talking more about God's blessing on helping the poor in Chapter 15.

Question 10

"God would never curse anyone simply for shutting his eyes to the needs of the poor."

–FALSE. Webster Defines the word "curse" as: "a calling on God or the gods to send evil or injury down on some person or thing." A curse is something that hinders God's blessings upon a person, family or church family. Deuteronomy 28 is a lengthy chapter detailing both the blessings of obedience and the curses of disobedience on God's people. The word "curse" is found hundreds of times in the Bible, literally from Genesis to Revelation. Many evangelical churches don't like to study the subject, but it is real. Disobedient, professing believers have brought curses upon themselves. I believe the same could be said about disobedient church families – bringing curses on themselves and hindering the blessings of God. Proverbs 28:27 clearly says that those who shut their eyes to the poor will have many curses. Our God is also our Heavenly Father. He desires to bless His children if we will meet His condition of obedience. I am also a father and I desire for my children and my eight grandchildren to be blessed. Father God cannot violate His Word. The truth is that thousands of local churches, many professing to be Bible believing, are closing their doors for ministry every year. Showing God's love to the poor and needy is one way to receive the blessings of God and avoid the many curses for those who chose to shut their eyes.

Question 11

"Sodom was judged by God primarily for their sin of immorality."

–FALSE. Ezekiel 16:49 was a shock to me when I really read it. It says, *"Behold, this was the guilt of your sister Sodom: she and her daughters had arrogance, abundant food and careless ease, but she did not help the poor and needy."* **Think of it!** Sodom was not judged by God primarily for their sin of immorality, as I was always taught. God judged Sodom for having abundant food and refusing to share it with the poor and needy. I used to be proud of not smoking, not drinking, and not doing this and that. Even though God doesn't want us to do certain things harmful to

224

our body, He is looking for people who will do His will in helping others in need.

Question 12

"God guarantees His people in the Old Testament will never be judged by Him simply for not treating the poor and needy properly."

–**FALSE.** Amos 4:1, 2 says, *"Hear this word, you cows of Bashan who are on the mountain of Samaria, Who oppress the poor, who crush the needy, Who say to your husbands, 'Bring now, that we may drink!' The Lord God has sworn by His holiness, Behold the days are coming upon you when they will take you away with meat hooks, and the last of you with fish hooks.'"* One of the themes of the books of the prophets, from Isaiah to Zechariah, deals with the treatment of the poor. God treats the poor fairly and He expects His people to do the same. God promises in Amos 2:4-7 to send judgment on His people for selling the poor into slavery. In Amos 4:1, 2, God promised judgment again against His people for oppressing the poor and crushing the needy. God promises more judgment in Amos 5:11 for imposing heavy rent on the poor along with charging them high taxes. God promised in Amos 8:7 that He would never forget the evil deeds of His people against the poor. God guarantees His own people will be judged if they treat the poor, whom God created and loves, unfairly. The worst mistreatment of the poor is to act like they don't even exist. The poor are to be sought out and loved by God's people. Much of the American church has turned helping the poor over to the government. Human government has its place but it isn't equipped by God to preach the gospel, disciple the believer and provide for all basic needs – spiritually and physically. Only a loving church can do this task. I pray God will spare His judgment against His people who don't care.

Question 13

"Jesus would never expect His followers to help the poor and needy just because He did it."

–**FALSE.** The Great Commission given in Matthew 28:18-20 includes making disciples in all nations. This includes Jews and Gentiles, rich and poor, bond and free, without regard to race, creed or color. Jesus expected His followers to observe what He commanded them to do. He commanded His followers to love God, and to love their neighbors as themselves. This means getting out of your "comfort zone" to make a real difference. Jesus promised to be with us as we obey His commands to love.

Question 14

"Jesus said preaching the gospel to the poor was not an evidence of Him being the Messiah."

–**FALSE.** Luke 7:22 says, *"And He answered and said to them, 'Go and report to John what you have seen and heard: the blind receive sight, the lame walk, the lepers are cleansed, and the deaf hear, the dead are raised up, the poor have the gospel preached to them.'"* Jesus gave six proofs of Him being the Messiah to encourage John the Baptist who was getting ready to die for his faith. Jesus listed preaching the gospel to the poor on the same supernatural level as opening blind eyes or raising someone from the dead. All the mighty miracles Jesus performed, as well as preaching the gospel to the poor, was a result of the Holy Spirit anointing Him to do so. Preaching the gospel to the poor was a first priority of Jesus. It should be a first priority of those who bear His name.

Question 15

"Jesus said those who called Him Lord would not be held accountable for not helping the poor and needy; especially if they failed to recognize Jesus through the needs of the poor as long as they said helping the poor wasn't their calling."

-FALSE. For me, this is the saddest question of the 15 questions we have examined. Jesus is teaching from Matthew 25: 31-46 of the difference between a spiritual sheep and spiritual goat. He taught in the first part of this section that those who truly were the spiritual sheep of Jesus would do six things: Feed the hungry, give water to the thirsty; take in strangers; clothe the naked, visit the sick, and visit prisoners in prison. Those who were spiritual goats would not recognize Jesus in performing these six acts of love to people in need. The spiritual goats even called Jesus "Lord" in verse 44. In verse 47 Jesus said these words: *these will go away into eternal punishment, but the righteous into eternal life."* We cannot earn our salvation by helping the poor and needy. Jesus said those who were truly righteous would demonstrate it by these six acts of kindness as if they were done directly unto Him. Those who had not demonstrated care for the poor and needy were not truly spiritual sheep. They were sent into eternal punishment. **Helping the poor is not optional.** Someone once sent me a nice check with the words, "I'm glad that God hasn't called me to help the poor." Everyone doesn't have to serve the poor and needy at Love Church. Every true believer is to help the poor everywhere.

Review

How did you do on your answers for the 15 questions offered in this chapter? I don't think my answers would have been the same before Fran and I began to work with the poor and needy many years ago. I never realized that even people who call Jesus "Lord" face potential judgment from Jesus. This is stated in Matthew 25:47. I well remember as a child the sermons on hell from Matthew 25:41. Somehow the preachers I heard speak on that passage never finished the chapter. I am not trying to scare someone into serving the poor and needy but I know salvation involves more than just saying, "Lord, Lord." Jesus said in Mark 3:35, *"For whoever does the will of God, he is My brother and sister and mother."* God's saving grace is not an excuse for not doing God's will. God's saving grace has been given to us to equip us to do God's will, including providing a church home for the poor and needy. Biblically speaking, I don't know how anyone can live a victorious Christian life without obedience to the Word of God.

III John, verse 4 says, *"I have no greater joy than this, to hear of my children walking in the truth."* Jesus identified Himself in John 14:6 as, *"...the way, the truth and the life...."* Jesus not only taught truth –He was the truth. The truth is God loves the people of the inner-city and He will provide for those who show them His love.

Let's move on to Section V – "God's Plan for Effective Inner-City Ministry." In Chapter 12 we'll examine the importance of developing a vision for inner-city ministry. In Chapter 13 we'll examine the importance of developing partners in ministry. In Chapter 14 we'll examine the importance of city-wide church relationships. I trust God is speaking to your heart and mind about getting more involved with the needy.

SECTION V

GOD'S PLAN FOR EFFECTIVE INNER-CITY MINISTRY

CHAPTER 12

DEVELOPMENT OF A VISION FOR INNER-CITY MINISTRY

SCRIPTURES RELATING TO CHAPTER 12

DEVELOPMENT OF A VISION FOR INNER-CITY MINISTRY

Matthew 16:18 – *"...I will build My church and the gates of Hades will not overpower it."*

Proverbs 29:18 – *"Where there is no vision, the people are unrestrained, But happy is he who keeps the law."*

Luke 9:51 – *"...He was determined to go to Jerusalem."*

Acts 2:47a – *" And the Lord was adding to their number day by day those who were being saved."*

Acts 26:19 – *"So, King Agrippa, I did not prove disobedient to the heavenly vision."*

Philippians 1:1 – *"...To all the saints in Christ Jesus who are in Philippi.."*

Ephesians 4:16 – *"from whom the whole body, being fitted and held together by what every joint supplies, according to the proper working of each individual part,..."*

Revelation 5:9 – *"And they sang a new song, saying, 'Worthy are You to take the book and to break its seals; for You were slain and purchased for God with Your blood men from every tribe and tongue and people and nation."*

Genesis 12:4 – *"So Abram went forth as the Lord had spoken to him."*

CHAPTER 12

DEVELOPMENT OF A VISION FOR INNER-CITY MINISTRY

"A person without a vision will always return to his own past"
– A. R. Bernard

Webster defines the work "vision" as "something supposedly seen by other than normal sight; …the ability to perceive something not actually visible…"

Men and women that have been greatly used of God through thousands of years have been men and women of vision and God-ordained purpose. Noah spent 120 years building a boat because of the vision God gave him. Joseph was a man of vision who helped rescue his family, even after they mistreated him. Moses was a man of vision who, despite his human fears, led God's people out of Egypt. Joshua and Caleb were men of vision, trusting God to defeat the giants in the Promise Land. David was a man of vision, believing God to help him defeat the mighty giant. Queen Esther was a woman of vision, greatly used of God to help save the Jewish people from extinction. Nehemiah was a man of vision used of God to help rebuild the walls of Jerusalem. The Apostle Paul was a man who obeyed the vision for missions that God gave him. Jesus was obedient to the vision God had for Him. He was willing to go to Jerusalem and die for the sins of the entire world.

Proverbs 29:18 (KJV) says, *"Where there is no vision, the people perish…"* Proverbs 19:18 (NAS) says, *"Where there is no vision, the people are unrestrained…"* Everything and every created being has been given a vision from their creator. Every part of the human body has been given a function that no other part can fulfill. Leaders need a vision from God to be able to fulfill their purpose to lead their followers. It takes courage to know your vision and live it out. Jesus could say "follow me" because He was a man of vision and He knew where he was going. The church of Jesus

233

Christ urgently needs leaders who have a sense of vision to help bring the people into everything that God has for them.

My Personal Struggles in Having and Forming a Vision

I have shared briefly in other parts of this publication of my personal struggles because of not forming a vision for my life and ministry. Part of my struggle came from a lack of self-esteem. I would ask myself questions like, "How can a person know that they have a vision from God?" "Who am I that God would give me a vision – I'm nothing special." I thought God only gave vision and purpose to really important saints. I saw people claiming a vision from God but not living a consistent Christian life. I saw vision as legalistic and restrictive. I'm basically an informal guy. I don't need a vision. It sounded too spooky to me.

Jesus said in John 7:17, "*If anyone is willing to do His will, he will know of the teaching whether it is of God or whether I speak from Myself.*" According to John 8:28-29, Jesus received daily instruction on what His Heavenly Father wanted Him to say and where He wanted Him to go and who He wanted Him to help. Jesus promised His followers in John 16:13 that the Holy Spirit would guide them into all truth. Acts 16:6 says the Holy Spirit stopped Paul and his company from preaching the gospel for a time in Asia. He gave Paul a vision to go elsewhere.

God doesn't give us a vision and purpose just for us to fulfill our vision and purpose. God doesn't give us a vision to advance our kingdom, but to advance His kingdom. A person's purpose is why God placed them on this earth. It takes a vision to see and know your purpose. Vision and purpose go together well but they serve two different functions. A church family needs a clear vision from God to understand its purpose from God. God promised to guide us as long as we are seeking to know and to do His will for our lives. Let me tell you how God helped me to develop my vision.

234

Two Helpful Pastor Friends

I want to tell you about two pastor friends – Bob Yawberg and Ron Allen. These men were both greatly used of God to help me in the formation of the vision for Love Church. Let me just say that I pastored a church for 14 years without a vision. God used my sincere efforts for Him but things would have gone much more effectively if I would have earnestly sought God for my purpose and vision before we started Fellowship Bible Church. I want to challenge young pastors to learn from my mistakes, especially as it relates to a lack of purpose and vision for the ministry. I believe God will show a pastor their purpose and vision if they will earnestly seek out God and wise counsel. It is not up to another human being to determine a person's purpose and vision but God does supply wise counsel to confirm a person's purpose and vision. God gave me two good pastor friends who helped me greatly in this vital matter. A young pastor could learn a lot about vision simply by spending time with other pastors who have a strong sense of vision in their ministry. Pastor Bob Yawberg and Pastor Ron Allen are both men of vision. Pastor Yawberg has completed over 50 years in pastoral ministry including over 30 years in Fort Wayne. Pastor Bob has been used of God to help disciple many men into the pastoral ministry. He has helped to plant several local churches in the area. When Bob was in his early 40's, God was giving him numerical success with a fast growing church on the northwest part of Fort Wayne. They were looking at how to expand their physical facility. One day Bob was driving downtown and felt drawn to an old abandoned church facility on the corner of Broadway and West Wayne. The building was over 100 years old with beautiful stained-glass windows. There was no strong evangelical church downtown at that time. For three years church services had not been conducted in the building Bob was seeing.

To make a long story short, God gave Bob a vision to purchase the old West Wayne Street United Methodist Church building. Many of Bob's friends didn't understand why he would want to leave a successful church facility in a nice area and come downtown to a challenging neighborhood. As a result of God's vision for Bob and his congregation, Broadway Christian Church has been greatly used of God in the downtown community. We'll learn more about this urban ministry in Chapter 15. Thousands of lives have been influenced for God's kingdom by one obedient man who walked out God's vision for his church ministry.

Pastor Ron Allen is also a man of vision. He has been used of God to help plant many churches in his 40 years of ministry. This includes nearly 25 years in the Fort Wayne area. I can honestly say that no pastor has helped me more in the formation and development of the vision of Love Church than Ron Allen. I want to tell you how God has used him in my life. I was talking with Bob Yawberg one day back in 1986 about starting Love Church. He recommended that we both go see Ron Allen and get his input. I was impressed with Bob's humility, recognizing Ron's gifting for church planting.

Bob and I went to visit Ron in his office. I asked Ron if he felt I was ready to start Love Church. We had known each other for several years. He said something to me that I will never forget. He said, "Phil, you are not ready to start Love Church until you can tell me the vision of Love Church in one sentence." I did not like his statement but I knew God was speaking to me about vision through Ron Allen. I told him I would need some time and prayer to be able to state our vision in one sentence. Several weeks later I told him the vision of Love Church was to be: "A church family demonstrating Christ's love to the poor and needy." I asked him if that was ok with him. He said that he needed three other important things from me relating to our church vision. He asked me for a list of church priorities, personal priorities, and a list of things God didn't ask us to do. I thank God for his wise counsel.

236

Several weeks later I returned with a list of church priorities including:

1. Praise and Worship
2. Prayer
3. Teaching of God's Word
4. Fellowship with God's people
5. Outreach to those outside of Love Church

My Personal priorities were:

1. Me and God
2. Me and Fran
3. Me and my family
4. Me and Love Church
5. Me and the Body of Christ
6. Me and my world

I told him I didn't believe God called us to have a day care or school, or conduct VBS from our facility. Ron said it was important to know what you are not called to do so you don't spend time with non-essentials for your ministry. No church can do everything well no matter what the size. Each part of the body has a unique function to perform. Each local church family needs to do something well as a part of its function in the body of Christ. I believe God called Love Church to do two things well: To show the love of Jesus to the poor and needy and to build relationships of unity and cooperation with God's people across the community.

Summary

Although this chapter is short in length, it is very important. Having a clear, defined vision has made a tremendous difference in my life and ministry. The results of a church not having or losing its vision is very tragic.

Let's move on to Chapter 13, "Partners in Ministry," and see how God uses teamwork to accomplish His ministry, especially in the inner-city.

CHAPTER 13

<u>Partners in Ministry</u>

PARTNERS IN MINISTRY

Nehemiah 4:6 – *"So we built the wall and the whole wall was joined together to half its height, for the people had a mind to work."*

Nehemiah 6:15, 16 – *"So the wall was completed on the twenty-fifth of the month Elul, in fifty two days, When all our enemies heard of it, and all the nations surrounding us saw it, they lost their confidence; for they recognized that this work had been accomplished with the help of our God."*

Luke 10:1, 17 – *"Now after this the Lord appointed seventy others, and sent them in pairs ahead of Him to every city and place where He Himself was going to come." " The seventy returned with joy, saying, 'Lord even the demons are subject to us in your name."*

Acts 1:14 – *"These all with one mind were continually devoting themselves to prayer, along with the women, and Mary the mother of Jesus, and with His brothers."*

I Corinthians 3:5, 6 – *"What then is Apollos? And what is Paul? Servants through whom you believed, even as the Lord gave opportunity to each one. I planted, Apollos watered, but God was causing the growth."*

Acts 4:23 – *"When they had been released, they went to their own companions and reported all that the chief priests and the elders had said to them."*

CHAPTER 13

PARTNERS IN MINISTRY

I shared in Chapter 12 how two ministry partners helped me to develop the vision of Love Church. That vision is "To be a church family demonstrating Christ's love to the poor and needy." I would not have the ministry today that God has blessed me with if it had not been for many ministry partners that God has supplied over the years. I have heard that God does not bless pastors trying to be Lone Rangers. Even the Lone Ranger had Tonto for his partner. Jesus sent His disciples out two by two. Nobody gets anywhere in life without help from others.

God uses two people to make one baby. Noah had the help of his three sons to build the ark. Moses had Aaron and Hur as ministry partners in Exodus 17:12. They held up his hands which resulted in a military victory. David had military partners which helped him to win many battles. Peter and John were ministry partners greatly use of God in the book of Acts. The Apostle Paul had Barnabas and Silas at different times for his ministry partners. The ultimate ministry partnership is the eternal relationship between God the Father, God the Son, and God the Holy Spirit. God, Himself, said in Genesis 2:18 that it was not good for a man to be alone. The worst punishment prison officials can inflict is to put a prisoner in solitary confinement. It is so sad that many people in ministry have chosen to put themselves in a type of solitary confinement. Isolated people are not as effective as they can be working together in Christ-honored relationships. Nehemiah could have never rebuilt the ancient walls of Jerusalem by himself. A great miracle took place as humble servants worked in harmony with each other for a common Godly cause.

In this chapter we will examine three types of ministry partners: Prayer and accountability partners, hands-on teamwork partners, and support partners. Each person in ministry needs each type of partner to help address a different type of need. It's wonderful that

God uses all different types of people to serve as ministry partners. Let's first examine the role of prayer and accountability partners.

1. Prayer and Accountability Partners

Jesus said in Matthew 21:13 that His house shall be called a house of prayer. Jesus spent much time in prayer with His Heavenly Father. His disciples were chosen after a night in prayer. Jesus prayed in Mark 14:36, *"yet not what I will, but what You will."* That prayer led Jesus to pay for the sins of all mankind. The Church of Jesus Christ started as a prayer meeting (Acts 1:14). All through the Bible we see the importance of prayer both for individuals and for groups.

We'll be sharing more about group prayer efforts across Fort Wayne in Chapter 14. Le me just say a word of personal thanks to pastors like Jim Hines, Bob Yawberg, Doyle Staton, John Edwards and others who prayed with me and for me over many years. We had wonderful times pouring our hearts out to God and to each other early in the morning at Broadway Christian Church. We had some great times of food and fellowship after the prayer times. We would meet at the cafeteria of St. Joseph's Hospital just two blocks from Broadway Christian Church. I'll never forget when one of the pastors accidentally brought out the fire department when he got a piece of toast stuck in the hospital toaster, causing much smoke but little damage.

Praying together regularly obviously helped build some friendships which continue today after 30 years of partnership. Praying together reduces the feelings of isolation from one another. Some pastors pray very quietly. Some are more expressive in their prayers to God. Prayer partners help to balance each other out. We have learned to appreciate prayer traditions that differ from our own. It is amazing that God answers prayer of people who are different from us. Praying together faithfully helped us to work together in areas of common cause such as abortion, pornography, racial issues, justice system, schools, and helping the poor.

Praying together helps us to see the things that unify us are much stronger than the few things that divide us. Most importantly, we believe praying together brings joy to the heart of our Heavenly Father. His people can be one as the Father and Jesus are one. Praying together is a win/win effort.

In 1993 I attended a meeting of pastors in New Paris, Indiana. I received a notice that H. B. London would be speaking to several hundred pastors. Fran was able to go with me. Pastor London shared on the subject of accountability. I had a lot of pastor friends but I was not in accountability with any of them. I had some bad experiences when I pastored Fellowship Bible Church in the area of legalism. I didn't know the difference between legalism and accountability. I would later discover that legalism and accountability are worlds apart. I did know that I did not ever desire to return to legalism.

I do not claim God is speaking to me very often but I do know God was speaking to me during Pastor London's presentation about accountability. The worst part was that God told me that I needed to seek out a pastor named Jim McCarty about the possibility of him and me becoming accountability partners. Pastor McCarty and I came from the same legalistic background. I went back to the book table after Pastor London's presentation and almost fell to the floor in shock. Pastor Jim McCarty was standing right in front of me! I didn't know that he was even in attendance. We had little contact with each other prior to the New Paris Conference. I told Jim that I needed to talk to him about the possibility of being his accountability partner. I was struggling with the idea of being accountable to him. I told him some things that I know he would disagree with just to see his reaction. He was very understanding and we agreed to meet on a twice-monthly basis. It wasn't long before Tom Dyer joined us. Dave Swineheart and Don Dennie joined us shortly thereafter. We had such a great time that we decided to meet together once a week. It's the best thing a pastor can do for himself, his family, and his ministry; to be in accountability with loving, supportive pastors. We don't have to agree with each other in every area, but we have to be willing to listen to each other. We have to be willing to be honest. We have to make our times of accountability a real priority in our weekly schedule. We can talk about anything; and we do. The one rule is that what is shared here, stays here. Our group is not primarily a prayer group but we do make a sincere effort to pray for one another's requests.

We have had other pastors join us for short periods of time. Some have moved on to other areas of pastoral service. Some have to work either part-time or full-time in addition to their pastoral duties. There is no paper work to fill out. It is all based on mutual love and respect for each other. Some pastors have come and desired to debate some political or theological issue. We just let them know that we are not there to debate but to develop relationships that will build up one another and advance God's kingdom in Fort Wayne.

I shared earlier that God took Jim McCarty to heaven on February 1, 2007. I still miss him greatly. I can honestly say that we never had a harsh word between us in our 14 years of accountability. I am so grateful to him and my other accountability partners for the vital role they have played in my life, family, and ministry.

Accountability Changes and Restores

We have seen lives and ministries of pastors changed through loving relationships developed through accountability to one another. It has been a great blessing to see the lives and ministries of pastors also restored over the years. I have witnessed relationships restored which were nothing short of a miracle. Due to privacy issues, I cannot go into detail but I will say there are some pastors that are still in ministry today primarily because of the loving relationships developed through accountability. My own life is a witness to accountability. Fran's life has been blessed by the fact that her husband is in accountability with other Godly men. Pastor McCarty was always available to also talk with Fran when she needed to talk.

The Bible is a book of accountability. God, Himself, is accountable to His written Word. Jesus is accountable to the Father. The Holy Spirit is accountable to both God the Father and God the Son. The disciples were accountable to Jesus in Luke, Chapter 10. Peter and John were accountable to their church family in Acts 4:23. The Apostle Paul was accountable to the other leaders after completing his mission journey.

Recent figures indicate that approximately 1,500 pastors in America are quitting the pastorate each month. There is much to be discouraged about in our society. There are many problems inside and outside the church walls that pastors have to face daily. The sad fact is that many pastors would rather quit the ministry than to be open to accountability; Accountability that could be used of God to help save their ministry. I've seen pastors who have felt like giving up the ministry receive encouragement through the loving relationships of pastoral accountability and are still faithfully serving today.

Pastor friend, let me ask you three questions. Who has God given you to be your accountability partner? Who do you meet with on a regular basis to share your joys, burdens, and needs? To whom are you reaching out to build pastoral friendships of accountability? Pastors desire their people to be accountable to their leadership. We model that need for accountability by having it ourselves. I John 3:16 tell us that Christians are to lay down their lives for one another. Accountability on a regular basis is one of the ways we put this verse into practice. It is my observation that the majority of pastors do not enjoy the benefits of regular, consistent times of pastoral accountability. Encourage your pastor to develop such a relationship. It has made such a difference in my life and in the life of my family and inner-city ministry.

2. Hands-on Teamwork Partners

The most common term found in the Bible to describe a leader is the word "servant." Moses, Joshua, David, Paul, James and Jesus, among many others, were described as servants. I Corinthians 3:5 tells us, *"What then is Apollos? And what is Paul? Servants through whom you believed, even as the Lord gave opportunity to each one."* Whatever success our inner-city ministry has enjoyed has come from the understanding that God has called us to be His servants, one to another. Being a true servant, according to Jesus, is a high calling (Matthew 20:27). Servanthood must first be modeled by the pastor and his wife. I'm honored to have Fran as my marriage partner and true servant to our ministry.

Being a Godly servant to others is a constant emphasis on our ministry. The word "demonstrate" in our church vision needs to be a part of every true Christian's life style. I often preach and teach on the subject of being a servant in response to God's love toward us. I would say that almost seventy per-cent of the people who come to Love Church on a regular basis are involved in some type of service. Many of our people do not have much in financial wealth but they can serve one another. We provide 30 to 40 different ways our people can get involved in servanthood at Love Church. We probably drive a lot of people away with our emphasis on serving. We tell people there are many places to attend church where they can just sit and do nothing. Love Church is not such a church home. Love in a practical way means to serve. We try to live up to our name – Love Church – but we all fail from time to time. We are seeing slow but steady progress in developing a team of working servants within our church family.

We also attempt to develop servants outside of our local church family. We encourage everyone to get involved in serving within the inner-city, regardless of their church family. We have been blessed with a number of fine youth groups who volunteer as work-teams to do various tasks for our ministry. These kids help clean our large facility, maintain our grounds, pass out bread to our needy neighbors, conduct neighborhood children's ministry, and many other important acts of service for us. We have skilled workers who help to build items, repair items, and install items for us. Qualified painters help us out from time to time. We have skilled workers help make quality items in our wood shop. We've had people work on our roof, help with heating and air-conditioning, and help clean our floors. Our 43,000 square foot facility is well maintained. Many visitors are amazed at how attractive our facility is on the inside. Our meeting place is a converted warehouse. Prior to our purchase in 1997, workers used to make mattresses and later made boats in our building. It takes a lot of hands-on teamwork partners to help make our ministry possible. No person can do inner-city ministry alone.

3. Support Partners

It takes an amazing amount of support of all kinds to have an effective inner-city ministry. I spend at least one-third of my time building relationships outside of Love Church. I average at least one speaking engagement per month to a variety of church families. This is needed to keep the vision and needs of Love Church before others. I count it a real privilege to minister to other church families about the needs that Love Church is attempting to meet in the inner-city. Most evangelical Christians have little understanding of the inner-city and its needs. I see God using our ministry as a bridge between those inside and those outside of the inner-city. Many churches never saw the inner-city as a mission field until they started working with Love Church. It has been a real joy to work together with God's people across many denominational and racial lines. Even after being in town over 37 years, many Christians have still not heard of us or visited our facility even one time. We have a lot of work to do to get the word out that God loves the people of the inner-city and will provide for those who show them His love. Love Church is a testimony to God's love for the poor.

People often ask us, "What does Love Church need?"

We answer that question is in one word, "Everything". People first getting involved often start by bringing clothes to us.

We are one of the few places in town that doesn't charge for the clothing. We have to operate both a winter clothing ministry and a summer clothing ministry. Doris Poling is assisted by Bob  and Sue Harter and helped by other volunteers in this vital ministry.

We feed many hungry people in the course of a year. Many  churches will have food drives for us. Most Christians offer to help with food primarily from Thanksgiving until Christmas. We have discovered that people need food twelve months a year rather than just four weeks a year. We need pastors who will purchase one food bag for each member in their church family and challenge their people to help fill these bags three to four times each year. Churches working together can help provide a lot of food items for needy and hungry families.

We also provide hot meals for all children on Sunday morning and sack lunches for them on Sunday night and again at our Thursday night service.

Often people will donate furniture, appliances, and household items. These are a real blessing to those who have that need. Thanksgiving and Christmas provide a great opportunity to show Christ's love to the needy. We have churches that faithfully provide Thanksgiving baskets. The busiest time of the year is, of course, Christmas. In 2006 we were able to adopt 175 needy individuals for Christmas. In 2007 were able to adopt 276 needy individuals for Christmas. It is a blessing for me to sit down on Christmas morning and know that our ministry has generously donated to help make a Merry Christmas for others in need. This can only be accomplished by the cooperation of many parts of God's family. Although not all of the poor and needy show the proper gratitude, we know God is pleased when His people demonstrate His love through giving and that's enough for us.

The final means of needed support is financial support. Many years ago when our ministry was first getting started, I was complaining about the need I had to raise financial support. I had a wise advisor who told me, "Phil, if you are going to work with the poor, you better learn to be at peace with the fact that you will have to raise funds for that privilege." Want to know a secret? It takes money to conduct an effective urban ministry. Currently our yearly church budget is $300,000.00. We have to raise about two-thirds of that total from concerned individuals outside of our Love Church family. We have some wonderful financial givers who attend Love Church but our people could never raise the needed funds. Outside support is greatly needed.

My dad used to tell a silly story. A donut maker makes donuts for a living. It cost him ten cents to make a donut and he sells it for five cents. How long will it take for him to make a profit? The answer is never. If we work with the poor and it costs us $3.00 per person and each give $1.00, how many poor people will it take for a ministry to make a profit? The answer, again, is never. In fact the more poor people that a church ministries to, the more funds it will have to raise. I encourage every church family to put the inner-city in your church budget. We are in constant need of church families to put Love Church in their annual mission's budget. We would be glad to show you our church budget so you can see what we are doing with the funds that God gives us.

Nobody is getting rich at Love Church but I honestly believe that we are doing what God has called us to do. We have two major fund-raisers a year to help us make our budget. Each year in the spring we have our annual fund-raising banquet. Last year we had Christians from 50 different church families attend. We invite a good speaker with a real heart for urban ministry. We also have different people from our ministry give their testimonies how God has used the ministry of Love Church in their lives. This banquet is always a high point of our church year. It is like a big reunion of faithful supporters. We have volunteers who help prepare a delicious dinner for us. We only charge $10.00 per person and everyone knows we will be taking up a free-will offering to help us with needed future expenses. The other major fund-raiser for the year is the annual Labor Day walk-a-thon held at Foster Park in Fort Wayne. We have people from many different churches that help us raise needed transportation funds. We encourage youth groups to walk with us. One pastor friend of mind rode his bicycle 100 miles to help raise needed funds for us. Other church families have fund raisers for us, like concerts, throughout the year.

Fund raising is a very necessary part of effective inner-city ministry. Sometimes I feel like a beggar with a tin cup reaching out to others. I must be willing to ask others and trust God to speak to hearts about helping to meet our needs. God has supplied our needs but I have to be willing to ask for help whether it be clothes, food, appliances, workers, or finances. I believe in what we are doing and I know God always provides through His people. Thanks to all of you who are helping us to make a difference in many needy lives by showing God's love in a host of practical ways. Let me know personally if there is any other way that God may be leading you in how He wants you to be involved.

We move on to one of my favorite subjects in Chapter 14 –City-wide church relationships. There is much ignorance among Christians concerning this matter. My desire is to honor God through His City-Wide Church in Fort Wayne.

CHAPTER 14

CITY-WIDE CHURCH RELATIONSHIPS

SCRIPTURES RELATING TO CHAPTER 14

CITY-WIDE CHURCH RELATIONSHIPS

Psalms 133:1-3 – *"Behold, how good and how pleasant it is For brothers to dwell together in unity! It is like the precious oil upon the head, Coming down upon the beard, Even Aaron's beard, Coming down upon the edge of his robes. It is like the dew of Hermon Coming down upon the mountains of Zion; For there the Lord commanded the blessing--life forever."*

Acts 8:8 – *"So there was much rejoicing in that city."*

Romans 1:7 – *"to all who are beloved of God in Rome, called as saints:'*

I Corinthians 1:2 – *"To the church of God which is at Corinth,..."*

I Corinthians 12:13 – *"For by one Spirit we were all baptized into one body, whether Jews or Greeks, whether slaves or free, and we were all made to drink of one Spirit."*

Galatians 3:28 – *"There is neither Jew nor Greek, there is neither slave nor free man, there is neither male nor female; for you are all one in Christ Jesus."*

Ephesians 4:4 – *"There is one body..."*

Colossians 1:2 – *"To the saints and faithful brethren in Christ who are at Colossae; Grace to you and peace from God our Father."*

I Thessalonians 1:1 – *"To the church of the Thessalonians in God..."*

CHAPTER 14

CITY-WIDE CHURCH RELATIONSHIPS

*"Jeremiah 29:7 – "Seek the welfare of the city where I have
sent you into exile, and pray to the Lord on its behalf; for in
its welfare you will have welfare."*

One of my primary motivations for writing this book is to let my
readers know of the Biblical concept known as the "City-wide
Church." I am so grateful that Love Church is a local church but
also a part of the city-wide church. The City-wide church is a
church that God is bringing together for His good and for His
glory. Our ministry would never be what it is today without being
a part of the city-wide church. Let's look into God's Word and see
what it says about it.

Let me say that from my early years in church until God opened
my eyes, I never heard of such a term as the "city wide church"
preached or explained. I knew our local church was a church. I
knew of the universal church comprised of everyone who believed
in what we believed. It was only many years later that I learned to
appreciate what God was doing in the city-wide church. God says
in Psalms 133 that it is good for brothers to dwell or live together
in unity. Why does God say it is good? First of all, it is good for
God to see His children living in harmony with one another. God
is a father and no father desires to see his children fighting with
each other or even worse, ignoring one another. Fran and I have
two children and it was a blessing to see them truly getting along
with each other as they grew up. It broke our hearts when, at
times, our children did not get along. Division among children
comes when they both feel they are individually right and the other
child in the family is wrong. Parents recognize that when children
are fighting with each other that they are probably both wrong. It
must grieve our Heavenly Father to see the number of local
churches divided by pride and unforgiveness. Jesus knew a
divided house could not stand. Second of all, dwelling together in

unity is good for the children involved. They enjoy a sense of peace, working toward common goals, bringing honor and joy to the parents.

Let's look at the background of Jeremiah. In Jeremiah 29:4 he says that God sent His people into exile from Jerusalem to heathen Babylon as a punishment for their disobedience. This punishment lasted 70 years. In Jeremiah 29:5, God told His people to build houses in Babylon and live in them. He further instructed the Jewish people in exile to plant gardens and build families. He challenged the people to seek the welfare of the city and pray to the Lord on its behalf. He said, in effect, as the city is blessed you will be blessed.

I believe God's desire for His people, exiled in Babylon, is the same desire today in every city. He desires for us to build houses, plant gardens, have fruitful families, and most of all pray to the Lord on the city's behalf. So often Christians don't have what I call a city-wide viewpoint. They only see their part of the city as important. They think, "As long as God blesses our part of the city, sorry about yours." We need Christian leaders from every part of our city to work together and pray together seeking God for the city's welfare. Some leaders are primarily concerned about social issues. Others are concerned about spiritual matters, government matters, educational matters, financial matters, recreational matters or other areas that affect the quality of life in our community.

We need Christians involved in every area affecting our community, whether it be the arts, jobs, police, justice system, community development or a host of other important concerns. We recently had elections in Fort Wayne to choose a new mayor. I was privileged to meet with a group of pastors and with each of the candidates. It was good to hear their viewpoints and for us to express our viewpoints. The most important thing we did was to pray with each candidate. Now that the election is over, we intend to meet with our new mayor and pray again with him. We had the former mayor attend several of our yearly banquets. We have had a good relationship with our city and it has blessed our ministry. For too long Satan has tried to isolate the church influence to just Sunday mornings. We need to be salt and light to our community seven days a week.

Jesus talks to preachers

"A new commandment I give to you, that you love one another, even as I have loved you, that you also love one another. By this all men will know that you are My disciples, if you have love for one another."

John 13:34, 35

One of the pastor leaders of Fort Wayne over the past 40 years was an African-American by the name of Reverend Jesse White. He pastored True Love Missionary Baptist Church for many years prior to his death several years ago. Jesse and I became good friends over the years. He was a well know civil rights leader and was very kind and generous to me. I preached in his church several times. He invited me to be his guest on his daily radio broadcast. He had big sideburns. He also had a great laugh that he exercised frequently. He brought his great choir to our tent crusade that we hosted in the 1970's. He was greatly used of God to help build low cost housing. Shortly before his death, I was able to show him our computer ministry. I told him that he was the one who gave me the idea for having a computer ministry.

One day I was talking with him about John 13:34, 35 and the need for Christians to show more love to one another. He told me something I will never forget about that passage of scripture. He said, "Jesus was talking to preachers." Jesus was talking with His disciples who were trained to become preachers. Jesse said that when the preachers start showing love to one another, then the world is going to start listening to our message. Even the enemies of Jesus recognized His love for Lazarus in John 11:36. Love is hard to argue against. Someone may say, "Puppy love isn't real." Someone else may say, "Puppy love is real to the puppy." I thank

God for the Fort Wayne area pastors that love me. I am constantly trying to build new relationships of love; reaching out to every pastor I can. I praise God for these relationships. I have heard many of them say to me that I was the first pastor to contact them when they moved to Fort Wayne. Reaching out to pastors is just as important to me as loving the people attending our local church.

Let's look further into God's Word and see what it has to say about a city-wide church. Luke 10:1 says, *"Now after this the Lord appointed seventy others, and sent them in pairs ahead of Him to every city and place where He Himself was going to come."* Jesus set the pattern by ministering in one city after another. Philip was sent to minister in the city of Samaria according to Acts 8:5. As a result, God moved in a mighty way throughout the city; resulting in deliverance, a mighty healing, and God's Word being preached. Acts 8:8 says, *"so there was much rejoicing in that city."* This is God's will for every city; to be impacted by His Word and His miracles.

The Apostle Paul addressed the city-wide church in many different cities. He addressed his letter to all who are beloved of God in Rome. He further wrote to the church of God which is at Corinth. Church history tells us there were approximately 60,000 believers in Corinth. They obviously didn't meet in one large meeting place. They met throughout the city. Paul refers to them as the church of God which is at Corinth. The same man who wrote in the twelfth chapter of I Corinthians, verse 13 which says, *"For by one Spirit we were all baptized into one body...'* sternly corrected the Corinthian city church in I Corinthians 11:17-34. He spoke about some who would attempt to bring division by identifying themselves with one leader instead of the whole church. There are approximately 1,500 different denominational groups in America. All claim the title of "Christian". A survey was taken of missionaries who have chosen not to return for a second tour of foreign missionary service. These Christian missionaries were asked to state the number one reason for not returning to the mission field. The answer shocked me. It wasn't the weather, living conditions, language barrier, finances, or even bugs and snakes. The number one reason given for not returning was that they couldn't get along with the other missionaries. Our Heavenly Father desires to display His goodness, but division within our city has hindered the city-wide church from impacting our needy community.

Paul's desire for unity and cooperation was expressed in I Corinthians 1:10. He wrote, *"Now I exhort you, brethren, by the name of our Lord Jesus Christ, that you all agree and that there be no divisions among you, but that you be made complete in the same mind and in the same judgment."* He wrote in Galatians 3:28 that all believers have been *"baptized into one body."* And in Ephesians 4:4 *"There is one body..."* Paul wrote to all the saints in Christ Jesus who are in Philippi (Philippians 1:2). He further wrote to the city-wide church in Colossus and Thessalonica. John wrote to seven city-wide churches found in the 2nd and 3rd chapters of Revelation, including the city-wide church in Ephesus, Smyrna, Sardis, and Philadelphia. Colossians 4:16 indicates that Paul instructed his letters to be read to the church of the Laodiceans. Paul loved all believers and he desired that all believers be instructed from his inspired writings.

If Paul was alive today in your community, who would he desire to instruct? Who would he desire to exclude of those naming Jesus Christ as their Savior and Lord? Who would he desire to be effectively used of God to bring the gospel of Jesus Christ? Would he be happy to know that many pastors have no interest in building relationships outside of their individual group? Would he be happy to know of professing Christians speaking against other Christian groups without even speaking to one another?

When Jesus said in Matthew 16:18 that He would build *"My Church,"* I can guarantee you that He had more in mind than your local church or even your denominational group. Let me ask you a serious question. If God's Word says there is only one body, what body does He recognize in your community? The Church of Jesus Christ is described in Revelation 21:2 as a *"bride adorned for her husband."* Here's another question – How many brides does Jesus have? The wonderful answer is one. He has one church in the city. He has one church in the universe. It's time for the city-wide church in your community and in my community to build relationships that will advance God's kingdom.

How Does The City-Wide Church Work?

Pastor friends who attended our 2007 banquet

There are many ways that a city-wide church can effectively work together. I believe the foundation for a successful city-wide church must start with prayer. Prayer helps us understand God's heart and desire for our city. Prayer helps to build relationships of trust and accountability. Prayer is used of God to help produce genuine humility showing us that we need one another. Prayer opens our hearts to one another. Prayer serves as the door for our needs to be met both individually, as a local church, and as a city-wide church. Prayer puts us all on the same level; praying to the same God and His Son, Jesus Christ. Prayer leads us to worship and praise God no matter how differently we express ourselves through styles and responses. Prayer helps us to appreciate one another which brings glory to God. Prayer helps to build city-wide

260

relationships; bringing needed changes to a community that honors the Lord.

I have been privileged to be involved with city-wide prayer efforts in Fort Wayne for nearly 35 years. I have seen how city-wide prayer efforts have brought the walls of division and suspicion tumbling down. Through united prayer efforts in Fort Wayne, pornographic book stores, adult movie theaters, and many illicit massage parlors have been closed. We are making some progress in the area of racism. It is still a major problem in our community. Relationships of genuine friendship are being built and sustained through praying for and praying with one another. Fort Wayne is a better community because of the prayer efforts of His people.

I have been personally involved and blessed to be a part of a city-wide church prayer movement though the ministry of Fort Wayne Renewal Ministries. We get together as men in ministry once a month; excluding the month we journey to Holland, Michigan for a four day prayer summit and again in December due to the hectic holiday schedule.

The men in ministry meet in the morning for about three hours at various sites throughout our community. Ladies in ministry also meet monthly; also at various sites. On the first Monday evening of each month, couples in ministry gather for a Dutch-treat meal at a local restaurant. Over a period of time, real relationships and friendships are being built among men and women in ministry. Hundreds and hundreds of invitations are sent out on a regular basis inviting various community leaders. We don't want to exclude any professing believer. Leaders need each other and we need to pray for and with each other.

Some people criticize this city-wide movement of prayer. They say, "All you people do is pray." The honest truth is that prayer is a great ministry to the Lord all by itself. In addition, God uses our prayers to accomplish His will within our community. As a result of prayer, friendships are being formed. These friendships are leading to times of joint ministry. Hundreds of us have marched together to see the sin of racism defeated in our community. We have fed thousands of hungry people over the years by combining our resources for this worthy cause. Several years ago a local pastor's son was shot by a stray bullet. As a result of relationships, built on prayer and cooperation, many area Christians fasted to see God do a miracle in this young man's life. Today he is active and well.

I thank God for Pastor Monte and Diane Sheets, who have given unselfish leadership to this city-wide church prayer effort. I thank God for Cedarville Community Church and for their encouragement and support of Monte and Diane in these efforts. There are no membership forms to complete to join. Everyone is welcome to attend and be involved. I thank God for the men and women who give leadership to this worthy relational cause by serving as servant-leaders. We continue to seek God on how we can be more effective in building city-wide church relationships and advancing God's kingdom in the greater Fort Wayne area.

Love Church – Blessed By Others

I am including in the back of this book (Appendix A) is a list of partnering churches and a list of business partners and ministry partners. I am making this list available because I am truly grateful to everyone who has helped to make our ministry of showing Christ's love to the poor and needy possible. I am sorry if the name of your church, business or ministry was missed. It was unintentional. Paul tells us in II Timothy 3:1, 2 that people will be, among other things, ungrateful in the last days. I believe we are living in the last days. Romans14:7 says, *"For not one of us lives for himself, and not one dies for himself."* I remember singing the words to a song we sang in a school choir, "No man is an island, no man stands alone." We live in the most independent country in the world. Sometimes this feeling of independence comes into the church and produces an "I don't need you" attitude. Paul reminds us in I Corinthians 12 that the various parts of the body cannot say to one another, "I don't need you."

Another reason for producing these two lists of Love Church partners is to encourage the reader, especially pastors, to build city-wide church relationships of prayer and friendship. Take a look at the partnering church list and see the variety of people from the various churches that are helping us. We don't agree on every doctrinal point. Frankly, I would have some major adjustments if God led me to attend some of these churches on a regular basis. We all believe, however, that God loves the poor and that His Church needs to be involved making a difference in the lives of hurting people. Our business and ministry partners have also been a great source of provision and encouragement to us. God bless you.

Let's move on to Section VI. I have entitled this simply as "Summary." In Chapter 15 we will see God's promise of blessings on inner-city ministry. I trust God is showing you how you and your church family can really make a difference in the inner-city. I'm excited about bragging about God's goodness to us.

SECTION VI

SUMMARY

CHAPTER 15

GOD'S PROMISE OF BLESSINGS ON INNER-CITY MINISTRY

GOD'S PROMISE OF BLESSINGS ON
INNER-CITY MINISTRY

Deuteronomy 28:1-3 – "*Now it shall be, if you diligently obey the LORD your God, being careful to do all His commandments which I command you today, the LORD your God will set you high above all the nations of the earth. All these blessings will come upon you and overtake you if you obey the LORD your God: Blessed shall you be in the city, and blessed shall you be in the country.*"

Psalms 1:1-3 – "*How blessed is the man who does not walk in the counsel of the wicked, Nor stand in th epath of sinners, nor sit in the seat of scoffers! But his delight is in the law of the Lord, And in His law he meditates day and night. He will be like a tree firmly planted by streams of water, which yields its fruit in its season and its leaf does not wither; And in whatever he does, he prospers.*"

Proverbs 19:17 – "*One who is gracious to the poor man lends to the Lord, And He will repay him for his good deed.*

Proverbs 28:27 – "*He who gives to the poor will never want, But he who shuts his eyes will have many curses.*"

Luke 6:38 – "*Give, and it will be given to you…*"

Luke 14:13, 14 – "*But when you give a reception, invite the poor, the crippled, the lame, the blind, and you will be blessed since they do not have the means to repay you; for you will be repaid at the resurrection of the righteous.*"

James 1:25 – "*…and effectual doer, this man will be blessed in what he does.*"

CHAPTER 15

GOD'S PROMISE OF BLESSINGS ON INNER-CITY MINISTRY

Acts 20:35 – "In everything I showed you that by working hard in this manner you must help the weak and remember the words of the Lord Jesus, that He Himself said, ' It is more blessed to give than to receive.'"

The word "weak" in this verse is defined as "to be feeble in any sense, be diseased, impotent, and sick or to be made without strength." I heard the last part of this verse about the blessings of giving quoted many times right before offering time. Many preachers leave out the first part of the verse that relates to the specific type of people that the church needs to help in order to be blessed. It's amazing to me that God loves the poor and needy and He will provide for those who show them His love. This book is not written primarily to the poor and needy. It is written primarily to the church of those professing Jesus Christ as their personal Savior and Lord. It is written to help God's people understand that God has obligated Himself to provide for those who show the poor and needy of His love for them. I can humbly say that Love Church is a testimony to God's provision and blessing upon His work. One pastor who is experienced in working with the poor and with God's blessings upon his ministry said, "If a church doesn't have any poor people coming to their church services, rent them out. Pay them $5.00 an hour to sit in your services." It was meant to be funny but it was a great statement of Biblical truth. After all these years of working with the poor and needy I don't completely understand why God loves these dear people so much, but I know He does. Why does God supply over a billion dollars annually to support the Salvation Army? Why has He provided, for over 100 years, for places like the Pacific Garden Rescue Mission in Chicago? I believe it's because they are ministering to the poor and needy. In contrast, many church families are in serious financial trouble today. I've seen 35 local churches in Fort

Wayne close their doors since Fran and I arrived in 1970. The majority of churches are stagnant; experiencing little spiritual or numerical growth. Many churches have lost their sense of mission and purpose for their existence. I want to tell you of several different churches that have experienced God's blessings as they include the poor and needy in their missions outreach. Prepare to be blessed.

Church Number One

Without Walls International Church
Tampa, Florida

Senior Pastor: Randy White
Age: 50
Age of Church: Founded 1991
Type of Church: Charismatic/Pentecostal
Membership: 24,000 (started with 5 in attendance)
Missionary Budget: $0.80 of every dollar goes to Outreach
Missions.

I first heard about the church from our good friends Mike and
Darlea Moon who live in Carthage, North Carolina. We watched
an interview that Pastor Randy White gave on a Christian
television station. He talked about his church meeting in a large
tent in Tampa, Florida. He described a church family comprised of
thousands of people from a very diverse population. I was amazed
at how a church could grow to such a large size in such a short
period of time. I was blessed to hear of their outreach across many
class and racial barriers in the Deep South. I told Fran that I
wanted to visit their church and learn from them.

We went to Tampa for our first visit. When we arrived at this huge
outreach center, we were greeted by some very friendly parking lot
workers. The worship was exciting and the people acted like they
were happy to be there. Pastor Randy's message was Biblical and
practical. For many years I struggled with demonic thoughts such
as: "Phil, you cannot expect a church family to include people of
different races and different classes." After our first visit I knew
God was encouraging me with our ministry in Fort Wayne. I
brought a group of people from Love Church to visit the church in
Tampa. This visit got their spiritual batteries charged. We were
especially blessed to witness young people being involved in the
pink truck ministry. Volunteers brought these pink trucks into the
most run-down sections of Tampa. These trucks were modified so
that a platform could be folded out with PA equipment to reach the

271

neighborhood. I found out later that the church has over 200 outreach ministries to the poor and needy. We were told by one of the leaders to, "Eat the chicken and spit out the bones." I'm sure people could find some bones in their ministry. The truth is there is a whole lot of good chicken at Without Walls International Church. I would strongly encourage my readers to visit the church and see the many ways WWIC is impacting their community for Christ. You have been a blessing to me.

Church Number Two

Broadway Christian Church
Fort Wayne, IN

Senior Pastor: Jason Baeuerle (Pastor for 3 years)
Age: 34
Age of Church: Founded 1974
Type of Church: Interdenominational
Attendance: 400 on Sunday morning
Proposed Missions Budget: $55,380 (In-As-Much Ministry
Budget to assist the poor and needy was $120,000.00 in 2007)

I have talked about Broadway Christian Church several times in this book. I honestly do not know of a church family that is doing more to help with the total needs of the poor and needy in Fort Wayne than Broadway Christian Church. I can tell you from personal experience that BCC was there for me and my family when we desperately needed them. The founder of the church, Bob Yawberg, has been a father to me since the passing in 1986 of my own earthly father. We have had a life-giving relationship with each other for over 35 years. I am also grateful to Kevin Duval and Ben Bouwers for their service at BCC and to the Mortensen family in particular. Although still young in age, Pastor Jason Baeuerle and his wife, Melissa, have been a real blessing to Fran and I. We have enjoyed good time of food, fellowship and sharing together. God has given you a great future.

I want to share some thoughts on the In-As-Much ministry of BCC to the thousands of poor and needy individuals across Fort Wayne. This ministry is headed up by my good friend, Alyn Biddle. Alyn has also served over the past 20 years or so as one of our faithful church advisors for Love Church. Their mission statement is "Building dignity and self worth through a relationship with Jesus Christ and personal responsibility." Every Monday, Wednesday and Friday a long line of poor and needy folks stand in line at Broadway Christian Church to receive various forms of needed assistance. A team of 32 volunteers (half outside of BCC) meet

273

individually with each person who shows up. Housing and food have accounted for two-thirds of the financial needs. Bus tickets make up the other one third. There are currently ten churches, including Love Church, assisting in their good effort. I would encourage my readers to contact Alyn Biddle for more details on how your church can get involved. You may contact him at (260)423-2347 ext. 310

Church Number Three

Wallen Baptist Church
Fort Wayne, IN

Senior Pastor: John Suciu (Pastor for 20 years)
Age: 47
Age of Church: Founded 1954
Type of Church: General Baptist
Attendance: 750
Youth Pastor: Rob Mansfield (Trace and Pam Bowles are helping with the youth)

The relationship between Love Church and Wallen Baptist Church has only been developed over the past two years. Despite the relative short time of working together, I can honestly say that it has been a blessing to both congregations. Rich Coulter and I were visiting Fort Wayne area churches on the North side of town, when we first visited Wallen Baptist Church. We entered their building and met Mary Henry and told her of our ministry to the poor and needy. She told us that her husband had recently retired and was looking for something worth-while to do. As it has turned out, Bill Henry has been a wonderful blessing to us serving in the Love Community Center. This volunteer has faithfully helped our needy individuals develop their reading, computer and GED skills.

Larry Mueller from WBC has been a blessing volunteering to drive our church vehicles once per month to pick up needy folks to attend our church services. He has also gone with Dennis Kelly and me several times to visit Christian men in prison. Larry is just fun to be around.

Rob Mansfield, the youth pastor, called me last summer and told me that they were interested in bringing 25 to 30 young people and stay in our inner-city facility for four days to learn about urban ministry. He promised to bring some good adults who could help supervise the outreach effort. We had a great time together. These young people were wonderful. They did everything we asked them to do. Fran and I were amazed. We honestly didn't hear one complaint from any of these young servants. They helped clean the building, pass out bread to needy residents, put on a Vacation Bible School for our neighbors, greeted our Sunday morning visitors and assisted in the Sunday morning service. They have since returned many Thursday nights throughout the year to assist with our children's and youth ministry. Thanks Wallen Baptist – you are a blessing to us.

Church Number Four

Grabill Missionary Church
Grabill, IN

Senior Pastor: Bill Lepley (Pastor for 12 years)
Age: 55
Age of Church: Founded 1902
Type of Church: Missionary Church
Attendance: 774
Missions Budget: $328,262

Pastor Bill has been effective with our people because of his background. Jesus Christ changed his life completely. He is a good example to hurting people.

There are not too many churches that have Amish horse and buggies driving past their church facility. Grabill Missionary Church in the heart of Amish Country in Grabill, Indiana is just such an exception. Grabill is located approximately 15 miles northeast of Fort Wayne. This large, well established congregation has a good balance of young and old alike.

Acts 1:8 gives us a four-part calling to missions that Grabill Missionary Church has taken very seriously over the years. Jesus said that after His followers receive the power of the Holy Spirit that they are to be His witnesses in Jerusalem, all Judea, Samaria and the remotest part of the earth. Let's take a closer look at each of these four areas of needed missionary service.

Jesus said Jerusalem must come first. You start from where you are. Grabill Missionary Church has recently completed a large addition to their facility expanding their outreach to their nearby community. It has been a blessing to be invited to their neighborhood outreach carnival. This carnival touches over 1,000 people every August. Judea is next. This speaks to the surrounding communities. Grabill Missionary Church has helped to pioneer new churches in the area. Samaria is the area which many Christians avoid and it symbolizes the inner-city. Grabill Missionary Church has partnered with Love Church over the years helping to pay fifty per-cent of the salary of Rich Coulter who has been greatly used of God along with his wife, Lynn, who helps teach our youth. Grabill Missionary Church has supported foreign missionaries all over the world for many years. Grabill Missionary Church and Woodburn Missionary Church both have a mission's ministry to all four areas mentioned in Acts 1:8. Thanks, Grabill Missionary Church, for partnering with us. We look forward to a great future as we work together in God's kingdom. Let me challenge other church families to be like Grabill Missionary Church and sponsor an urban missionary.

Woodburn Missionary Church
Woodburn, IN

Senior Pastor: Joel DeSelm(Pastor for 20 years)
Age: 55
Age of Church: Founded 1906
Type of Church: Missionary Church
Attendance: 800
Missions Budget: $200,000 (Includes foreign, home and
benevolence giving)

I have said it before and I will say it again, no church family has
been more supportive of Love Church than Woodburn Missionary
Church. Pastor Joel and I received our master's degrees in
Christian Ministry from Huntington College in Huntington,
Indiana. This is where we started our friendship which has lasted
over 20 years. To compare our two church families, we have little
in common but our love for Jesus Christ as expressed through the
poor and needy.

Woodburn Missionary Church is big, traditional, denominational
church comprised of largely stable, rural Christians. Love Church
is much smaller, non-traditional and comprised of a combination of
stable and unstable urban Christians. We have been having unity
services together for almost 20 years. When we first started to
worship together, I heard a prayer given by a man named Lester
Schlatter who is now with the Lord. He prayed, "God bless our
sister-church, Love Church." I will never forget that prayer by that
Godly saint. Despite our many outward differences, we are family
in ministry together. I always try to tease Woodburn Missionary
Church about the "Free Manure" sign out on Highway 14 just prior
to where we turn onto Highway 101 to Woodburn.

Woodburn Missionary Church provided $28,000.00 back in 1997
to help us purchase our current facility at 1331 East Berry Street.
They have also provided regular donations of mission funds, food,

clothes, household items and project workers. I think the most important thing they have provided is a great sense of friendship. Two couples in the church allow Fran and me to stay two weeks a year at their beautiful condo at Hilton Head, South Carolina. Pastor Joel has been a wonderful advisor and friend to me. Fran and I had the privilege of going to Israel with Pastor Joel and his sweet wife, Judy, in 2006 along with several other good friends from Woodburn Missionary Church. Thanks Woodburn Missionary Church for all you mean to us at Love Church. I pray other churches will follow your kind example.

God Blesses the Faithful

God has promised over and over in the Bible to bless His obedient servants. He tells us in Deuteronomy 28:3 that those who obey His commandments will be *"Blessed...in the city, and blessed shall you be in the country."* The Psalmist tells us in Psalms 1 that the righteous man will prosper in whatever he does. In the book of Proverbs we see God's promises of blessings over and over to those who show His love to the poor and needy. Jesus tells us clearly in Luke 6:38, *"Give, and it will be given to you..."* Jesus further states in Luke 14:13, 14 that those who honor the poor will be blessed and repaid. James 1:25 tells us that the effectual doer of God's Word, *"..will be blessed in what he does..."*

I honestly do not want my book to be a commercial for Love Church. I deeply desire to brag on God's provision for those attempting to show His love to the poor and needy through His Church. I have enclosed several pages of facts and figures at the end of this chapter to show God's goodness to us. We are not a mega-church, even thought we have been blessed with many large churches who have been very kind to us over the years. Our first Sunday morning attendance in 1987 was 15 people but God was good to help us keep going during many times of challenge and discouragement.

I have attempted to show God's kindness to us through the five church families mentioned earlier in this chapter. I could have used many more church examples but neither time nor space will allow. I just want to encourage every church to know that they can make a real difference in the inner-city. Frankly, there is no real lasting help for the inner-city apart from caring, Christ-centered churches. I get frustrated with the church at times but I still believe the church has an important part to play in the inner-cities of our nation. I want to continually thank every Christian, every church and every person for helping us to make a real difference in the inner-city. The fact is that the Fort Wayne inner-city is better off today because of people who have chosen to make a difference by getting involved.

Del Allen, an old friend from Fellowship Bible Church had a great description of a wealthy person. He said, "A wealthy person is someone who has all his bills up to date, fifty cents in his pocket and no one is fighting over it." Love Church has all our bills up to date, more than fifty cents in the bank and no one is fighting us for it.

I want to brag on God's goodness to us in our ministry of showing Christ's love to the poor and needy. During 2007 we were blessed by God to do the following:

- Provide 25,000 loaves for bread distribution. Many church families joined together to pass out bread to our neighbors..

Preparing for bread give-away

- Provide a wonderful Christmas meal for 220 individuals on Christmas Sunday.

- We were able to provide 70 Christmas baskets and adopt 276 people for Christmas.

- We were able to provide food for 5,000 meals at the carnival give-away; provide food for 1,224 people from the food boxes plus provide hot meals for 1,214 kids on Sundays and sack lunches for 2,600 individuals on Sunday nights and 2,600 on Thursday nights.

- We were also able to provide school bags for 26 students; 76 Christmas stockings; 107 Thanksgiving baskets and free clothing the last six months of this year to 1,000 needy individuals.

- Our transportation ministry provided 3,965 rides in 2007 including 212 rides for people confined to wheelchairs.

- We had a fourteen per-cent increase in our Sunday morning services and a thirteen per-cent increase in our Sunday evening services and our Thursday evening services continue to grow.

- We had 599 first-time visitors attend either a Sunday morning or Sunday evening service. This comprised of 301 males and 298 females for the year. This is amazing because many inner-city churches have three to five times the number of females in attendance compared to males. We have a growing number of men in attendance.

- It cost over $32,000.00 to operate our transportation ministry in 2007. It cost us $8.07 per rider to provide transportation to and from our church services. We are blessed to have a good group of drivers, assistants and mechanics to help us in this ministry.

- Most importantly we have seen a number of our people receive spiritual help; including 21 people baptized into Christ during the year.

- We have supported home and foreign missions through 19 various projects; including sending a number of our children to Stillwater Camp during the summer.

The purpose of this chapter is to demonstrate the faithfulness of God to those attempting to show His love to the poor and needy. As the old hymn goes, "all I have needed, thy hand has provided, Great is Thy faithfulness, Lord unto me." Each of the five churches mentioned in this chapter have been blessed of God for their obedience in a team effort to minister to the inner-city.

I could tell you of miracle after miracle of God's provision for Love Church and for the Mortensen family. Check out the next two pages and see how our overall support has continued to grow over the years. Who ever heard of a landlord who never increased the rent once in 12 years and gave the tenant $10,000.00 as a parting gift? We were blessed with such a landlord that we only saw once in 12 years. I remember the day that we received a check for $100.000.00 from someone who wanted to help us purchase our 1331 East Berry facility. I have never met the generous giver who later gave an additional $50,000.00 to help cover the remodeling costs on the second floor.

This book is not really about one local church or even a city-wide church. It is a book attempting to describe God's love for the poor and the needy and His ability to provide for them through His people. As a young person, growing up in church, I could never picture myself working in the inner-city. Now I can't imagine working any place else. I felt so bad for traveling missionaries who had to go from church to church attempting to raise needed support. I told God I would never go around begging for needed funds. Now part of my calling is to challenge God's people to provide for the poor and needy and expect a blessing in return. These blessings may be a spiritual blessing, a material blessing, or just the blessing of knowing that Almighty God is using you to make a difference in someone's life. I know Love Church is making a difference and that's a great blessing to me.

In the final chapter I share ten challenges that any person must face if they are going to be fruitful in urban missions. I call urban missions "The Forgotten Church." The inner-city has been largely forgotten by many professing Christians. I thank God that He hasn't forgotten about the inner-city. He has promised to bless those who face the challenges and faithfully attempt to show His love to the poor and needy.

The figures on the graph on the following page show our actual working income versus the budgeted income. This graph does not show the following:

- In 1997 an additional $359,000.00 was received to purchase the facility at 1331 E. Berry. This made the total income $522,196.00.

- In 2007 an additional $129,409.15 was received to pave our parking lot. This made the total income $455,356.78.

September 1986 – December 31, 2007

Church Budget Needs	$3,084,700.00
Total Income	$4,271,830.57

GOD HAS PROVIDED OVER ONE MILLION DOLLARS OVER OUR BUDGETED NEED SINCE WE BEGAN! PRAISE GOD!

ACTUAL VS BUDGET

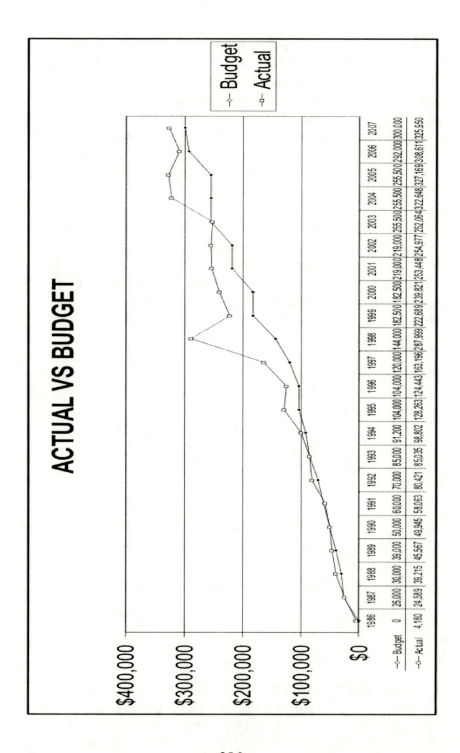

	1986	1987	1988	1989	1990	1991	1992	1993	1994	1995	1996	1997	1998	1999	2000	2001	2002	2003	2004	2005	2006	2007
Budget	0	26,000	30,000	39,000	50,000	60,000	70,000	85,000	91,200	104,000	104,000	120,000	144,000	182,500	182,500	219,000	219,000	255,500	255,500	255,500	292,000	300,000
Actual	4,180	24,589	39,215	45,567	49,945	58,063	80,421	85,035	98,802	128,263	124,443	163,196	297,999	222,686	239,821	253,448	254,977	252,064	322,648	327,169	308,611	325,950

—◇— Budget
—□— Actual

First-Time Visitors

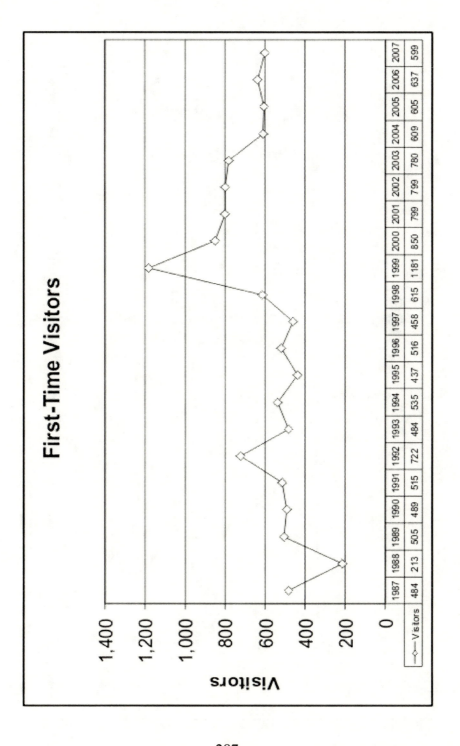

	1987	1988	1989	1990	1991	1992	1993	1994	1995	1996	1997	1998	1999	2000	2001	2002	2003	2004	2005	2006	2007
Visitors	484	213	505	489	515	722	484	535	437	516	458	615	1181	850	799	799	780	609	605	637	599

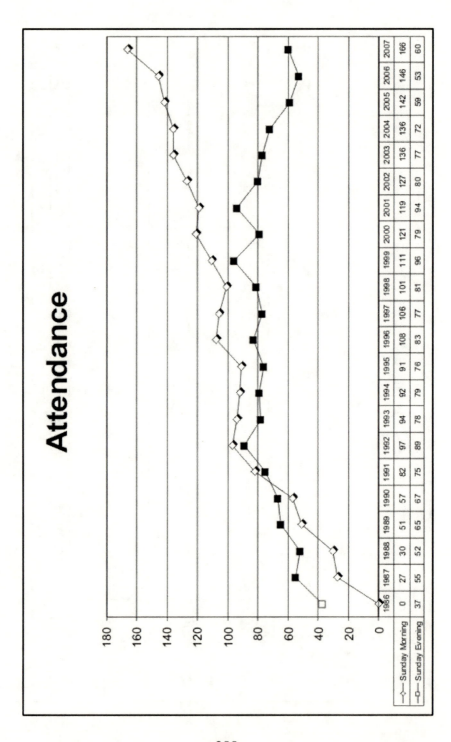

Attendance

	1986	1987	1988	1989	1990	1991	1992	1993	1994	1995	1996	1997	1998	1999	2000	2001	2002	2003	2004	2005	2006	2007
Sunday Morning	0	27	30	51	57	82	97	94	92	91	108	106	101	111	121	119	127	136	136	142	146	166
Sunday Evening	37	55	52	65	67	75	89	78	79	76	83	77	81	96	79	94	80	77	72	59	53	60

SECTION VII

CONCLUSION

CHAPTER 16

GOD'S CHALLENGE – URBAN MISSIONS: THE FORGOTTEN CHURCH

GOD'S CHALLENGE – URBAN MISSIONS:
THE FORGOTTEN CHURCH

Mark 16:15 – *"And He said to them, 'Go into all the world and preach the gospel to all creation.*

Acts 1:8 – *"but you will receive power when the Holy Spirit has come upon you; and you shall be My witnesses both in Jerusalem, and in all Judea, and Samaria, and even to the remotest part of the earth.'"*

John 4:9 – *"Therefore the Samaritan woman said to Him, 'how is it that You, being a Jew, ask me for a drink since I am a Samaritan woman?'"*

Acts 10:13 – *"A voice came to hem, 'Get up, Peter, kill and eat!' But Peter said, 'By no means, Lord, for I have never eaten anything unholy and unclean.' Again a voice came to him a second time. 'what God has cleansed, no longer consider unholy.'"*

Acts 10:27, 28 – *"As he talked with him he entered and found many people assembled. And he said to them, 'You yourselves know how unlawful it is for a man who is a Jew to associate with a foreigner or to visit him; and yet God has shown me that I should not call any man unclean...'" "And he said to them, 'You yourselves know how ʾunlawful it is for a man who is a Jew to associate with a foreigner or to visit him; and yet God has shown me that I should not call any man unholy or unclean.'"*

CHAPTER 16

GOD'S CHALLENGE –URBAN MISSIONS:
THE FORGOTTEN CHURCH

*"I Corinthians 16:9 – "for a wide door for effective service
has opened to me, and there are many adversaries."*

**"God is using whatever upsets you in the church to bring
change to it." –T.D. Jakes**

The word "adversaries" as used in this verse in the Greek means to
lie opposite to. To be set over against. It means to withstand. For
this chapter I am going to use the word "challenges." Yes, there
are many blessings upon God's people who are determined to
show His love to the poor and needy. It would be nice to be able
to tell you that everything will go smooth for individuals of a
church family who are determined to show Christ's love to the
poor and needy. Unfortunately, such is not the case. The truth is
that there are many challenges in doing the will of God. The poor
and needy will not be shown God's love without dedicated effort
and courage. There will be sincere Christians who do not
understand why a person should be involved in urban ministry.
Many Christians have fallen victim to one or more of the 15 lies
that hinder effective inner-city ministry that I mentioned in
Chapter 11. It wasn't easy for Jesus to do the will of His Heavenly
Father. We, as His servants, have no right to expect to be treated
any better than how Jesus was treated. Satan has had his grip on
the inner-cities of our nation for generations and he is not going to
release his grip without a good fight of faith by God's people.
Much of the urban church has been largely forgotten or ignored by
American Evangelicals. It is a lonely road at times, when one is
trying to be faithful in showing God's love to many who are
forgotten by our society. I can encourage you that God has not
forgotten the poor and needy. The way God reaches out to any
group of people is to form church families who will demonstrate
His love and concern for them. The same principle works in any

293

nation and in any society regardless of race or class. I want to share ten challenges that are facing the church of Jesus Christ as it relates to urban ministry to the poor and needy. All I ask is that you will be open to God's Word and God's voice as He helps you to deal with your challenges. Praise God for the wide door open to us for effective service. May God help us not to run from our challenges as His people did when they ran from the giants that lived in the Promise Land. God is bigger than any challenge we may face as we serve Him.

1. The Challenge of Ignorance

Hosea 4:6 – "My people are destroyed for lack of knowledge.."

There is an old saying that goes, "What a person doesn't know cannot hurt him." It sounds nice, but it's a lie. The inner-city is hurting in America largely due to the ignorance of the evangelical church to its nature and its needs. I was raised in ignorance of the inner-city. The only thing I knew about the inner-city was that it was dangerous and to stay away from it. I didn't have any friends living in the inner-city and we didn't worship with any church from the inner-city. "Those" people stayed on "their" part of town and "we" stayed on "our" part of town. "Those" people worshipped in "their" kind of Christian churches and we worshipped in "our" kind of Christian churches. Even though both groups of people claimed to be evangelical Christians, we did not believe we had much in common. Ignorance of one another was the only thing we had in common between the people living in the inner-city and the people living in the outer-city.

There is another saying that goes "Ignorance is bliss." It is one thing to be ignorant of one another and another thing to choose to stay ignorant of one another. Several months ago I invited a fine young African-American pastor to speak in our church. He gave a wonderful message on the need to invite Jesus into one's life. He told us that he had to leave right after our church service because he had to drive a truck to Chicago and back to Fort Wayne. He was doing his best to pastor his church and work a full-time job as a truck driver. We had a good evening together and we are making plans to do it again. While he was speaking to the audience, God was speaking to my heart. He reminded me that it wasn't until I got into the military that I ever heard a message preached to me by a pastor of another race. We have many pastor friends from various racial backgrounds who are now associated with our ministry. I wish I would have been exposed to God's people from different racial backgrounds earlier in my life and ministry. We are cheating ourselves from a great blessing when we stay away from each other.

2. The Challenge of Fear

Matthew 25:25 – "And I was afraid, and went away and hid your talent in the ground. See, you have what is yours."

Any person or church ministry will have to learn to deal with fear if they are going to be used of God in urban ministry. We fear what we don't understand. After he sinned Adam was afraid of God, and tried to hide. Peter was afraid to acknowledge that he was a disciple of Jesus Christ. Following the resurrection of Jesus, all of the disciples were afraid of the Jews. Someone once said these words, "Fear not". These words are found 365 times in the Bible, one for each day of the year.

"Fear Not" doesn't mean to deny the existence of fear. It simply means to trust God despite unknown and unseen circumstances. Fear is the opposite of faith and we cannot please God apart from faith according to Hebrews 11:6. The servants who produced an additional five talents and three talents in Matthew 25 had to push through their fears, unlike the fearful servant who returned his one talent to his master.

A fruitful servant working in the inner-city will have to deal with a number of fears; including the fear of failure, the fear of rejection, the fear of one's own inadequacy, and the fear of being misunderstood. Humanly speaking it is risky to invest one's life in the inner-city. It took many years of working in the inner-city before many Christians began to support Fran and me in our ministry. You have to be willing to fail as I did and as I shared in Chapter 6. You will fail. The greatest failure, however, is to not make your best effort in the first place. Others will reject you for your efforts. Some may secretly feel jealous of you for your willingness to do something they are not willing to do. Every leader has had to deal with their inadequacies and the fear of being misunderstood. We are not responsible for the results of our ministry but we are responsible to trust God to help us to be obedient to Him, despite our fears.

3. The Challenge of Apathy

Revelation 3:15, 16 – "I know your deeds, that you are neither cold nor hot; I wish that you were cold or hot. So because you are lukewarm, and neither hot nor cold, I will spit you out of My mouth."

Webster defines apathy as, "lack of emotion, lack of interest; listless condition; indifference." I sincerely wish that apathy was not a major challenge facing the American church today; but it is. The majority of churches are not growing numerically or in spiritual fervor. It is interesting that the word "fervor" literally means intense heat or great warmth of emotion and zeal. Jesus had a zeal for His Father's House according to John 2:17. Zeal is the opposite of apathy. We, as God's people, need to have a zeal also for the things for which Jesus was zealous. He was tempted in every sin without sinning Himself. I believe apathy is a sin because it hinders God's work from being done. We cannot and we must not give in to our feelings if we are going to bring joy and honor to our God and His Son, Jesus Christ. Paul writes in Colossians 3:23, *"Whatever you do, do your work **heartily**, as for the Lord rather than for men."(Emphasis mine)* The great command is to love God with all your heart.

296

You cannot be used of God in the inner-city or anywhere else with a half-hearted effort. Inner-city people can spot a phony from miles away. I love to see people in the inner-city worshipping God. Many of them understand that true worship begins, first of all, in the heart. I have heard reports from all over the world how Christians, who have little finances and humble worship facilities, worship God for long periods of time with everything they have. Visitors often comment how happy our people are to be in church and to worship God. Often material concerns rob us of the joy of what is really important in life. As a child, one of my favorite hymns was entitled "There is Joy in Serving Jesus." Satan is a thief and he is trying to steal our joy and that leads to apathy. May God revive His Church resulting in ministry to all, including the inner-city.

4. The Challenge of Finances

Philippians 4:15, 16, 19 – "You yourselves also know, Philippians, that at the first preaching of the gospel, after I left Macedonia, no church shared with me in the matter of giving and receiving but you alone; for even in Thessalonica you sent a gift more than once for my needs. And my God will supply all your needs according to His riches in glory in Christ Jesus."

As I said before, recent figures indicate that literally thousands of pastors all across America are quitting the pastoral ministry each year. The number one reason given for leaving the ministry was over money. Literally thousands of local churches are experiencing tremendous financial struggles that hinder their outreach ministry. When a church faces financial struggle the first casualties of the budget crisis are often foreign missions and home missions.

Several years ago a large evangelical church was featured in a national newspaper. This particular church, located in Houston, Texas, said they had 18,000 members. The article revealed their missions budget to help the poor. The amount set aside to help the poor and needy was $36,000.00; **Think of it!** One of the largest evangelical churches in America is giving only $2.00 per member per year to show God's love to the poor and needy.

Many years ago a famous female atheist, who helped stop prayer in the public schools, made a statement that angered many conservative Christians. She said that the Bible was a bunch of junk. I am a conservative Christian but I believe any professing Christian or any professing church family that doesn't care about the poor and needy doesn't really believe the Bible.

We demonstrate our faith in God's Word, not primarily by our words, but by our obedience to God's Word. Financial giving is one of the key ways that we express our love to Jesus for who He is and what He has done for us. Paul promised the Philippian church that God will meet their financial needs because they were willing to meet his financial needs. God will not supply financial blessings to those who refuse to honor God in their financial giving and in their living.

5. The Challenge of Unbelief

John 20:25 – "So the other disciples were saying to him, 'We have seen the Lord!' But he said to them, 'Unless I see in His hands the imprint of the nails, and put my finger into the place of the nails, and put my hand into His side, I will not believe.'"

Jesus spoke many times on the importance of the positive power of belief and the negative power of unbelief. He said in John 3:18, *"He who believes in Him is not judged; he who does not believe has been judged already, because he has not believed in the name of the only begotten Son of God."* In John 3:36 the word "believes" equals the word "obey." Belief and obedience go together. Thomas said in John 20:25, *"I will not believe."* He was indicating that belief is a matter of the will. We only truly believe what we practice. Jesus believed God and obeyed Him as a result.

298

Ask yourself some honest questions:

- Do I truly believe God loves the poor and needy?

- Do I truly believe every Christian, including me, has a loving obligation to show God's love to the poor and needy as Christ modeled?

- Does God desire for Christian churches to be planted in the inner-city and urban areas as much as He does in the suburban and rural communities of our nation?

- Does God desire for me to be more involved in showing His love to the poor and needy?

- Does God desire for my local church family to be more involved in urban missions?

I cannot answer these questions for anyone but myself. I truly believe that I cannot answer "yes" to any of these five questions unless I am willing to get involved through a loving act of obedience on my part. It's not enough to be emotionally touched by the needs of the poor and needy. Matthew 9:36(KJV) said that Jesus was *"...moved with compassion..."* He not only felt sorry for the needy individuals He observed, but actively went about meeting their needs. That is true faith. As a church we need to cry out to the Lord with the words in Mark 9:24, *"...I do believe; help my unbelief."*

6. The Challenge of Dead Religion

Acts 10:28 – "And he said to them, 'You yourself know how unlawful it is for a man who is a Jew to associate with a foreigner or to visit him; and yet God has shown me that I should not call any man unholy or unclean."

I have knocked on hundreds and hundreds of the doors of inner-city residents over the years. We have passed out thousands of loaves of bread in a sincere effort to show God's love to the poor and needy. Often we will be asked, "Where are you from?" When we first started and mentioned the word "church", it brought many negative responses. We heard many stories from the poor and needy who tried to attend a church service and were met with less than a loving response. One man told me how a pastor met him at the church door. The pastor told him to go home and put on a tie because "we dress up here for Jesus."

The word religion literally means to bind something or someone. In Acts 10:27, Peter gave his testimony of being bound to a faith which outwardly cared little for anyone outside of their own group. Peter was rebuked in Galatians 2:11-13 by the Apostle Paul for his hypocrisy in dealing in different ways with people, depending on who he was with at the time. Those who treated the poor and needy differently from the rich as they entered a worship service were rebuked in the second chapter of James. James plainly declares in James 2:17, *"Even so faith, if it has no works, is dead, being by itself."* And in James 1:27, *"Pure and undefiled religion in the sight of our God and Father is this: to visit orphans and widows in their distress, and to keep oneself unstained by the world."* Pure religion is really what we practice, not just claim to believe.

We had a visitor approach our church door recently asking the greeter, "Isn't this the church that cares about people?" The greeter said that it was. Dead religion doesn't care, but God's love does care and seeks to meet the needs of others, regardless of background.

7. The Challenge of Loving

Matthew 11:19 – "The Son of Man came eating and drinking, and they say, 'behold, a gluttonous man and a drunkard, a friend of tax collectors and sinners!' Yet wisdom is vindicated by her deeds."

Jesus said in Matthew 22:37, 38 that loving is the greatest command. Therefore, it stands to reason that the greatest sin is the refusal to love. I came from a background that emphasized refraining from doing things like smoking, drinking, dancing, playing cards, movies or hanging around heathens, etc. Our emphasis was on what we couldn't or shouldn't do. I believe that to abstain from some of this negative conduct that I just mentioned was a good idea. The missing emphasis I observed was on the reasons why we should abstain from certain harmful activities. I reasoned that we should abstain because we might get caught and get into trouble. The real motivation for not doing a particular activity or for doing a particular activity should be to show our love for God and His people. Revelation 21:4 says, *"and He will wipe away every tear from their eyes;..."* I personally believe God will wipe away tears from the eyes of His professing people as a result of failure on our part to love God and love others.

In Matthew 11:19 Jesus was criticized by the religious community of His day for being a friend of tax collectors and sinners! This was a charge He never denied because He loved the hated tax collectors and sinners. In Luke 7:36-50 Jesus was criticized again for showing love to a woman only described as a sinner. In Luke 19:1-10 Jesus showed Zaccheus, the tax collector, love and salvation and the religious people of Jesus' day grumbled when they observed Him going to Zaccheus' house. Jesus was further criticized for loving and forgiving the woman found in the act of adultery. (John 8:1-11). Truly loving people is a real risk that Jesus demonstrated over and over again. We have to be such risk-takers to please our God.

8. The Challenge of Building Relationships

Galatians 6:10 – "So then, while we have opportunity, let us do good to all people, and especially to those who are of the household of the faith."

The Bible is a very relational book. Our God is a very relational God. He has commanded His people to show His love by building loving relationships. The earthly ministry of Jesus was primarily based on the relational development of his twelve disciples. Jesus said in Mark 3:35, *"For whoever does the will of God, he is My brother and sister and mother."* Brother, sister and mother are all relational terms. The Apostle Paul refers to himself as a father in I Corinthian 4:15. He spoke of the Christian believers in I Corinthians 4:14 as, *"...my beloved children."* He even refers to himself in I Thessalonians 2:7 as, *"...a nursing mother tenderly cares for her own children."* Paul further encourages the believers in Galatians 6:10 to do good to all people.

Often churches have a very limited target of outreach. I have actually had pastors call me and ask me if our church would take certain individuals off their hands. I was told that they just didn't "fit" into their church family. I am amazed that people created by God and loved by God are not welcome in certain church families. We insist the one thing required for a person to attend Love Church is that they must be breathing. I believe that God has blessed our open-door, open-heart policy.

Relationships take time to build. I remember working with a pastor who was having difficulties in his ministry. I encouraged him to have a Saturday morning breakfast –inviting men who would be interested in building a relationship with him. He was amazed that 18 men actually showed up. I asked him several months later how things were going in the area of building relationship with his seeking men. He told me that he was too busy to build relationships with them. He was fired by the church six months later. Everything that we do at Love Church is relational; whether it means building relationships with those inside our church, outside our church or with the city-wide church. Programs take less time than relationships but I believe building relationships is the only way to help build a fruitful ministry.

9. The Challenge of the Mind

Proverbs 3;5 – "Trust in the Lord with all your heart and do not lean on your own understanding."

The challenge of the mind is one of the most difficult things to conquer. God's Word tells us to trust God with all our heart and lean not on our own understanding. In ministry there is a constant battle between the heart and the mind. There is an old saying that goes "Stinkin' thinkin' leads to stinkin' drinkin'." I've got news for you. "Stinkin' 'thinkin'" leads to a stinkin' life and stinkin' ministry. That's why Paul encouraged the Philippian church in Philippians 4:8 to constantly think about the things that are right, lovely, and pure and anything worthy of praise. Proverbs 23;7 says, *"For as he thinks within himself, so he is."* Our thought life will go a long way to determine the fruitfulness of our ministry. Satan will mess with our mind if we give him access to it.

Becoming a Christian is an insult to the mind. Romans 8:7 says, *"because the mind set on the flesh is hostile toward God; for it does not subject itself to the law of God, for it is not even able to do so."* Financial giving to an unseen God does not make sense to the natural mind. I Corinthians 2:14 says, *"But a natural man does not accept the things of the Sprit of God; for they are foolishness to him; and he cannot understand them, ..."* Planting a new church ministry in the inner-city does not make sense to the mind. I have had more than one pastor tell me that I was crazy to waste my time attempting to minister in the inner-city. Love Church is an insult to the human mind, but praise God I am confident that He is using it for His glory and for His kingdom.

I Corinthians 2:16 says, *"...we have the mind of Christ."* Jesus had the mind of a servant as recorded in Philippians 2:6-8. He gave up His life so that we could receive God's forgiveness and new life in Him. Paul further wrote in Philippians 2:3 that believers are to have *"humility of mind regard one another as more important than yourselves;"* We urgently need God's help in

303

order for us to serve the poor and needy with both our heart and our mind.

10. The Challenge of the "Who" and the "Why"

John 8:28, 29 – "So Jesus said, 'When you lift up the Son of Man, then you will know that I am He, and I do nothing on My own initiative, but I speak these things as the Father taught Me. And He who sent Me is with Me; He has not left Me alone, for I always do the things that are pleasing to Him.'"

The challenge of the "who" and the "why" is the most vital thing I can share in this book on urban ministry. The "who" refers to the person we are serving. The "why" refers to the motivation or the reason we are serving the poor and needy. I attended a get-together for pastors. We were asked to share what was the best thing about our ministry. I heard a number pastors share how blessed they were to see Godly change is some of the lives of the people that were a part of their ministry. I rejoice also in changed lives, but that is not the most important part of ministry for me.

Jesus knew who He was serving and why He was serving. Jesus came to seek the will of His Heavenly Father and then do it. Jesus received instruction from the One who sent Him each and every day. He referred to His Heavenly Father over 100 times in the book of John, alone. His love for His Heavenly Father motivated Him to do the will of His Father. I do not believe Jesus got discouraged in John 6:66 when many of his so-called disciples withdrew from following Him. Jesus came to earth primarily to please His Father. He asked Peter three times in John 20, *"Do you love Me?"* After Peter said yes three times, Jesus told him to feed His sheep. We love the Shepherd and that is the motivation to take care of God's sheep.

People often ask me, "Pastor Phil, you never seem to get discouraged; Why?" My honest answer is that I don't get discouraged as long as I remember who I am serving and why I am serving. I am serving my Heavenly Father who has called me to demonstrate His love to the poor and needy. Because I love Him I want to do His will for my life. <u>The real challenge is to never allow the people to be the focus.</u> Serving God out of love will really help urban missionaries not to get discouraged in serving the poor and needy. It sounds simple, but it's vital to understand.

A Closing Word

John 13:17 (KJV) – "if ye know these things, happy are ye if ye do them."

Several years ago Fran and I ran into a lady from Fellowship Bible Church. We had not seen her in several years. She bluntly said to us, "Well, you look tired, but you look happy." That's a pretty good description of most of the Christian servants that I know who are working to show the love of Christ to the poor and needy in the inner-city. We may be physically, mentally, and emotionally tired at times, but we are happy.

We are happy because we believe we are bringing joy to our Heavenly Father in response to His call into urban ministry. I am personally happy because I have the privilege of working with my helpmate in a real team ministry. It grieves me to see pastor couples going in two different directions. God has shown me that I could not be used of God as I am without Fran's loyal support. I am happy that I have not had to sacrifice my marriage for my ministry.

I have said many times, "If there is a happier pastor in Fort Wayne, I have not met him." I am happy because God has given Fran and me a church full of good people at Love Church. There is a sense of Godly optimism among us. We share good times of laughter as well as honest times of pain and tears. I am also happy to be a part of the city-wide church mentioned in Chapter 14. God has given us a host of friends in Fort Wayne and across America and many support us.

305

Closing Prayer

Genesis 30:1 – "Now when Rachel saw that she bore Jacob no children she became jealous of her sister; and she said to Jacob, 'Give me children, or else I die.'"(emphasis mine)

I wrote this book out of my desire to be truly obedient to the One who has called Fran and me into urban ministry. God does love the poor and needy and He will provide for those who show them His love. Please pray sincerely about your involvement in urban missions: The forgotten church. The Evangelical church in America desperately needs to get more involved. We need prayer warriors that will pray, "Give your church the poor and needy lest we die!"

Anyone seeking further information relating to the ministry of Love Church of Fort Wayne may either write to us at our mailing address at 1148 Kinnaird Avenue, Fort Wayne, IN 46807, or by visiting our website at http://lovechurchfw.org or call us at (260)422-8961. All proceeds received from the first printing of this book will go entirely to the ministry of Love Church of Fort Wayne, Inc. Love Church also has speakers available to come to your church upon request. Please contact Pastor Phil Mortensen for further details.

APPENDIX A

Partnering Churches

1.   Aboite Lutheran
2.   Aldersgate U.M.C.
3.   Anchor Community (UBIC)
4.   Avalon Missionary
5.   Beacon Heights C of B
6.   Beacon Light Chapel –Churubusco, IN
7.   Bethlehem Lutheran
8.   Bible Baptist
9.   Blackhawk Ministries
10. Broadway Christian Church
11. Brookside Community
12. Carroll Community WC
13. Carroll Community Worship Center
14. Carroll Road Christian
15. Cedarville Community Church –Cedarville, IN
16. Central Church
17. Christ Church of Faith
18. Christ Temple Church
19. Christ's Church Georgetown
20. Christian Chinese Church
21. Christian Praise & Fellowship
22. Church in Fort Wayne
23. Church In Jesus Christ
24. Church of Good Shepherd –Leo, IN
25. Come2Go Ministries
26. Cornerstone Community –Kouts, IN
27. Crosspoint Community Church
28. Crossview Church –Grabill, IN
29. Dunfee Missionary
30. Eden Worship Center –Topeka, IN
31. Emmanuel Community (UBIC)
32. Epiphany Lutheran (ELCA)
33. Evangel Christian Center

34. Faith Baptist Church
35. Faith Methodist
36. Fellowship Missionary
37. First Assembly of God
38. First Missionary
39. Frieman Square Fellowship
40. Grabill Missionary, Grabill, IN
41. Grace Christian Church
42. Grace Episcopal
43. Grace Gathering –New Haven, IN
44. Grace Missionary –Celina, OH
45. Greater Faith Baptist
46. Harkenflo Ministries
47. Harvest Time Worship Center
48. Harvester Ave. Missionary
49. Heartland Community church
50. Hope Missionary –Bluffton, IN
51. Huntertown U.M.C., Huntertown, IN
52. Imago Dei Ministries
53. Kalida Family O.C. –Kalida, OH
54. Kingdom Door Christian Worship Center
55. Level 13 Church
56. Liberty Hills Church
57. Life Bridge Church
58. Lighthouse Assembly –Decatur, IN
59. Lighthouse Free Methodist
60. Maplewood Mennonite
61. Markle Church of Christ –Markle, IN
62. Moorepark Community –Three Rivers, MI
63. Mt. Calvary Baptist
64. My Father's House –Fort Wayne, IN
65. Nappanee Missionary –Nappanee, IN
66. New Covenant Worship Center
67. New Hope Methodist -Mecosta, MI
68. New Life Church of God
69. New Life Lutheran
70. North Leo Mennonite, Leo, IN
71. Northeast Christian Church

72. Northpoint Community Church –Ft. Wayne
73. Olive Branch UBIC Church
74. Open Arms Methodist
75. Pathway Community Church
76. Pine Hills Church
77. Pioneer Methodist, St. -John's, MI
78. Plymouth Congregational
79. Powerhouse Family W.C.
80. Praise Lutheran
81. Promise Lutheran
82. Queen of Angels Catholic
83. Salvation Army
84. Skyline Community Church
85. Sonrise Methodist
86. Southern Heights Baptist
87. Southwest Lutheran
88. St. Alban's Episcopal
89. St. Joseph Catholic
90. St. Mary's Catholic
91. St. Michael's Lutheran
92. St. Nicholas Orthodox
93. St. Vincent Catholic
94. The Chapel
95. The Gathering UMC –Harrison, MI
96. the Ridge Church –Fort Wayne, IN
97. Third Street Church of God
98. Till Road C. C.
99. Tree of Life Baptist Church
100. True Love Baptist
101. Union Baptist Church
102. Union Chapel (UBIC)
103. Wallen Baptist Church
104. Westview Alliance
105. Westwood Fellowship
106. Without Walls I.C. –Tampa FL
107. Woodburn Missionary, Woodburn, IN
108. Word of Liberty Church –New Haven, IN

Love Church Business Partners / Ministry Partners

1. Associated Churches
2. Barry Ellis, Accountant
3. BCC In-As-Much
4. Campus Ministries
5. Cancer Services of N. E. Indiana
6. Central States Enterprises
7. Charis House
8. Chippewa Hills Education Assoc.
9. Country Baskets –Grabill
10. Cummings Mid-States Power, Inc.
11. D & G Engineering
12. Dayton foundation Depository
13. Deister Machine Co.
14. Euell Wilson Center
15. Experior Corp.
16. F. W. Trade Exchange
17. Feeding The Nations
18. Flint & Associates
19. Fort Wayne Compactor
20. Friends of Bethany
21. Ft. Wayne Renewal Ministries
22. Ft. Wayne Rescue Mission
23. Geisleman & Brown, LLP
24. Gone Fishing Ministries
25. Helen Wilson House
26. Hochstedler Floorcovering, LLC
27. Huntington University
28. International House of Prayer
29. Inter-Varsity C.F.
30. JDL Construction
31. Longhorn Quarter Horses
32. Love-In-Deed
33. Master's Investment Group
34. Mays Pest Control
35. Mechanix Unlimited

36. Medical Education & Research
37. Mennonite Mutual Aid
38. Metro Youth Sports
39. Metzger Trucking Co.
40. Midwest tool & Die
41. Miller Heating & Air
42. Miracle Stables
43. Mustard Seed Furniture
44. Nemco Food Service
45. Parrish Leasing
46. Pastors in Prayer
47. Personal Touch Cleaners
48. Photobak Portrait
49. Rich's Auto Repairs
50. Rizzo Barber Shop
51. Sam's Club
52. Save Our Kids Outreach
53. Schenkel-Shultz, Inc.
54. Shepherd's House
55. Taylor University –Fort Wayne
56. Taylor University –Upland
57. Te & E Asphalt
58. Thrivent Financial
59. Tri-Star Trucking
60. Vincent House
61. Votaw Electric
62. West Michigan Conference, UMC
63. Window, Doors & More
64. Windsong Ministries
65. World Missionary Press

PERSONAL NOTES

Printed in the United States
110044LV00005B/1-93/P